£2.95.

✔ KT-461-930

/ WEEK LOAN.

City and Islington Sixth Form College
283-309 Goswell Road
London
EC1
020 7520 0652

**CITY AND ISLINGTON
COLLEGE**

This book is due for return on or before the date last stamped below.
You may renew by telephone. Please quote the Barcode No.
May not be renewed if required by another reader.

Fine: 5p per day

7 DAY
BOOK

A04578

EDITORIAL DIRECTOR Laurie Barnett
DIRECTOR OF TECHNOLOGY Tammy Hepps

SERIES EDITOR John Crowther
MANAGING EDITOR Vincent Janoski

WRITERS Ross Douthat, Susannah Mandel
EDITORS John Crowther, Dennis Quinio

CITY AND ISLINGTON
SIXTH FORM COLLEGE
283 - 309 GOSWELL ROAD
LONDON
EC1
TEL 020 7520 0652

£2.99.

Copyright © 2003 by SparkNotes LLC

All rights reserved. No part of this book may be used or reproduced in any manner
whatsoever without the written permission of the Publisher.

SPARKNOTES is a registered trademark of SparkNotes LLC

This edition published by Spark Publishing

Spark Publishing
A Division of SparkNotes LLC
120 Fifth Avenue, 8th Floor
New York, NY 10011

Any book purchased without a cover is stolen property, reported as "unsold and
destroyed" to the Publisher, who receives no payment for such "stripped books."

Please submit all comments and questions or report errors to www.sparknotes.com/errors

Printed and bound in the United States

ISBN 1-58663-394-5

A04578

A Prologue from the Bard

Brave scholars, blessed with time and energy,
    At school, fair Harvard, set about to glean,
From dusty tomes and modern poetry,
    All truths and knowledge formerly unseen.
From forth the hungry minds of these good folk
    Study guides, star-floss'd, soon came to life;
Whose deep and deft analysis awoke
    The latent "A"s of those in lit'rary strife.
Aim far past passing—insight from our trove
    Will free your comprehension from its cage.
Our SparkNotes' worth, online we also prove;
    Behold this book! Same brains, but paper page.
If patient or "whatever," please attend,
    What you have missed, our toil shall strive to mend.

CONTENTS

Context

THE MOST INFLUENTIAL WRITER in all of English literature, William Shakespeare was born in 1564 to a successful middle-class glove-maker in Stratford-upon-Avon, England. Shakespeare attended grammar school, but his formal education proceeded no further. In 1582 he married an older woman, Anne Hathaway, and had three children with her. Around 1590 he left his family behind and traveled to London to work as an actor and playwright. Public and critical acclaim quickly followed, and Shakespeare eventually became the most popular playwright in England and part-owner of the Globe Theater. His career bridged the reigns of Elizabeth I (ruled 1558–1603) and James I (ruled 1603–1625), and he was a favorite of both monarchs. Indeed, James granted his company the greatest possible compliment by bestowing upon its members the title of King's Men. Wealthy and renowned, Shakespeare retired to Stratford and died in 1616 at age fifty-two. At the time of his death, literary luminaries such as Ben Jonson hailed his works as timeless.

Shakespeare's works were collected and printed in various editions in the century following his death, and by the early eighteenth century his reputation as the greatest poet ever to write in English was well established. The unprecedented admiration garnered by his works led to a fierce curiosity about Shakespeare's life, but the dearth of biographical information has left many details of Shakespeare's personal history shrouded in mystery. Some people have concluded from this fact and from Shakespeare's modest education that Shakespeare's plays were actually written by someone else—Francis Bacon and the Earl of Oxford are the two most popular candidates—but the support for this claim is overwhelmingly circumstantial, and the theory is not taken seriously by many scholars.

In the absence of credible evidence to the contrary, Shakespeare must be viewed as the author of the thirty-seven plays and 154 sonnets that bear his name. The legacy of this body of work is immense. A number of Shakespeare's plays seem to have transcended even the category of brilliance, becoming so influential as to affect profoundly the course of Western literature and culture ever after.

Shakespeare wrote *Twelfth Night* near the middle of his career, probably in the year 1601. Most critics consider it one of his greatest comedies, along with plays such as *As You Like It, Much Ado About Nothing,* and *A Midsummer Night's Dream. Twelfth Night* is about illusion, deception, disguises, madness, and the extraordinary things that love will cause us to do—and to see.

Twelfth Night is the only one of Shakespeare's plays to have an alternative title: the play is actually called *Twelfth Night, or What You Will.* Critics are divided over what the two titles mean, but "Twelfth Night" is usually considered to be a reference to Epiphany, or the twelfth night of the Christmas celebration (January 6). In Shakespeare's day, this holiday was celebrated as a festival in which everything was turned upside down—much like the upside-down, chaotic world of Illyria in the play.

Twelfth Night is one of Shakespeare's so-called transvestite comedies, a category that also includes *As You Like It* and *The Merchant of Venice.* These plays feature female protagonists who, for one reason or another, have to disguise themselves as young men. It is important to remember that in Shakespeare's day, *all* of the parts were played by men, so Viola would actually have been a male pretending to be a female pretending to be a male. Contemporary critics have found a great deal of interest in the homoerotic implications of these plays.

As is the case with most of Shakespeare's plays, the story of *Twelfth Night* is derived from other sources. In particular, Shakespeare seems to have consulted an Italian play from the 1530s entitled *Gl'Ingannati,* which features twins who are mistaken for each other and contains a version of the Viola-Olivia-Orsino love triangle in *Twelfth Night.* He also seems to have used a 1581 English story entitled "Apollonius and Silla," by Barnabe Riche, which mirrors the plot of *Twelfth Night* up to a point, with a shipwreck, a pair of twins, and a woman disguised as a man. A number of sources have been suggested for the Malvolio subplot, but none of them is very convincing. Sir Toby, Maria, and the luckless steward seem to have sprung largely from Shakespeare's own imagination.

PLOT OVERVIEW

I N THE KINGDOM OF ILLYRIA, a nobleman named Orsino lies around listening to music, pining away for the love of Lady Olivia. He cannot have her because she is in mourning for her dead brother and refuses to entertain any proposals of marriage. Meanwhile, off the coast, a storm has caused a terrible shipwreck. A young, aristocratic-born woman named Viola is swept onto the Illyrian shore. Finding herself alone in a strange land, she assumes that her twin brother, Sebastian, has been drowned in the wreck, and tries to figure out what sort of work she can do. A friendly sea captain tells her about Orsino's courtship of Olivia, and Viola says that she wishes she could go to work in Olivia's home. But since Lady Olivia refuses to talk with any strangers, Viola decides that she cannot look for work with her. Instead, she decides to disguise herself as a man, taking on the name of Cesario, and goes to work in the household of Duke Orsino.

Viola (disguised as Cesario) quickly becomes a favorite of Orsino, who makes Cesario his page. Viola finds herself falling in love with Orsino—a difficult love to pursue, as Orsino believes her to be a man. But when Orsino sends Cesario to deliver Orsino's love messages to the disdainful Olivia, Olivia herself falls for the beautiful young Cesario, believing her to be a man. The love triangle is complete: Viola loves Orsino, Orsino loves Olivia, and Olivia loves Cesario—and everyone is miserable.

Meanwhile, we meet the other members of Olivia's household: her rowdy drunkard of an uncle, Sir Toby; his foolish friend, Sir Andrew Aguecheek, who is trying in his hopeless way to court Olivia; Olivia's witty and pretty waiting-gentlewoman, Maria; Feste, the clever clown of the house; and Malvolio, the dour, prudish steward of Olivia's household. When Sir Toby and the others take offense at Malvolio's constant efforts to spoil their fun, Maria engineers a practical joke to make Malvolio think that Olivia is in love with him. She forges a letter, supposedly from Olivia, addressed to her beloved (whose name is signified by the letters M.O.A.I.), telling him that if he wants to earn her favor, he should dress in yellow stockings and crossed garters, act haughtily, smile constantly, and refuse to explain himself to anyone. Malvolio finds the letter, assumes that it is addressed to him, and, filled with dreams of marrying Olivia

3

and becoming noble himself, happily follows its commands. He behaves so strangely that Olivia comes to think that he is mad.

Meanwhile, Sebastian, who is still alive after all but believes his sister Viola to be dead, arrives in Illyria along with his friend and protector, Antonio. Antonio has cared for Sebastian since the shipwreck and is passionately (and perhaps sexually) attached to the young man—so much so that he follows him to Orsino's domain, in spite of the fact that he and Orsino are old enemies.

Sir Andrew, observing Olivia's attraction to Cesario (still Viola in disguise), challenges Cesario to a duel. Sir Toby, who sees the prospective duel as entertaining fun, eggs Sir Andrew on. However, when Sebastian—who looks just like the disguised Viola—appears on the scene, Sir Andrew and Sir Toby end up coming to blows with Sebastian, thinking that he is Cesario. Olivia enters amid the confusion. Encountering Sebastian and thinking that he is Cesario, she asks him to marry her. He is baffled, since he has never seen her before. He sees, however, that she is wealthy and beautiful, and he is therefore more than willing to go along with her. Meanwhile, Antonio has been arrested by Orsino's officers and now begs Cesario for help, mistaking him for Sebastian. Viola denies knowing Antonio, and Antonio is dragged off, crying out that Sebastian has betrayed him. Suddenly, Viola has newfound hope that her brother may be alive.

Malvolio's supposed madness has allowed the gleeful Maria, Toby, and the rest to lock Malvolio into a small, dark room for his treatment, and they torment him at will. Feste dresses up as "Sir Topas," a priest, and pretends to examine Malvolio, declaring him definitely insane in spite of his protests. However, Sir Toby begins to think better of the joke, and they allow Malvolio to send a letter to Olivia, in which he asks to be released.

Eventually, Viola (still disguised as Cesario) and Orsino make their way to Olivia's house, where Olivia welcomes Cesario as her new husband, thinking him to be Sebastian, whom she has just married. Orsino is furious, but then Sebastian himself appears on the scene, and all is revealed. The siblings are joyfully reunited, and Orsino realizes that he loves Viola, now that he knows she is a woman, and asks her to marry him. We discover that Sir Toby and Maria have also been married privately. Finally, someone remembers Malvolio and lets him out of the dark room. The trick is revealed in full, and the embittered Malvolio storms off, leaving the happy couples to their celebration.

CHARACTER LIST

Viola   A young woman of aristocratic birth, and the play's protagonist. Washed up on the shore of Illyria when her ship is wrecked in a storm, Viola decides to make her own way in the world. She disguises herself as a young man, calling herself "Cesario," and becomes a page to Duke Orsino. She ends up falling in love with Orsino—even as Olivia, the woman Orsino is courting, falls in love with Cesario. Thus, Viola finds that her clever disguise has entrapped her: she cannot tell Orsino that she loves him, and she cannot tell Olivia why she, as Cesario, cannot love *her*. Her poignant plight is the central conflict in the play.

Orsino   A powerful nobleman in the country of Illyria. Orsino is lovesick for the beautiful Lady Olivia, but becomes more and more fond of his handsome new page boy, Cesario, who is actually a woman—Viola. Orsino is a vehicle through which the play explores the absurdity of love: a supreme egotist, Orsino mopes around complaining how heartsick he is over Olivia, when it is clear that he is chiefly in love with the idea of being in love and enjoys making a spectacle of himself. His attraction to the ostensibly male Cesario injects sexual ambiguity into his character.

Olivia   A wealthy, beautiful, and noble Illyrian lady, Olivia is courted by Orsino and Sir Andrew Aguecheek, but to each of them she insists that she is in mourning for her brother, who has recently died, and will not marry for seven years. She and Orsino are similar characters in that each seems to enjoy wallowing in his or her own misery. Viola's arrival in the masculine guise of Cesario enables Olivia to break free of her self-indulgent melancholy. Olivia seems to have no difficulty transferring her affections from one love interest to the next, however, suggesting that her romantic feelings—like most emotions in the play—do not run deep.

5

Sebastian   Viola's lost twin brother. When he arrives in Illyria, traveling with Antonio, his close friend and protector, Sebastian discovers that many people think that they know him. Furthermore, the beautiful Lady Olivia, whom he has never met, wants to marry him. Sebastian is not as well rounded a character as his sister. He seems to exist to take on the role that Viola fills while disguised as Cesario—namely, the mate for Olivia.

Malvolio   The straitlaced steward—or head servant—in the household of Lady Olivia. Malvolio is very efficient but also very self-righteous, and he has a poor opinion of drinking, singing, and fun. His priggishness and haughty attitude earn him the enmity of Sir Toby, Sir Andrew, and Maria, who play a cruel trick on him, making him believe that Olivia is in love with him. In his fantasies about marrying his mistress, he reveals a powerful ambition to rise above his social class.

Feste   The clown, or fool, of Olivia's household, Feste moves between Olivia's and Orsino's homes. He earns his living by making pointed jokes, singing old songs, being generally witty, and offering good advice cloaked under a layer of foolishness. In spite of being a professional fool, Feste often seems the wisest character in the play.

Sir Toby   Olivia's uncle. Olivia lets Sir Toby Belch live with her, but she does not approve of his rowdy behavior, practical jokes, heavy drinking, late-night carousing, or friends (specifically the idiotic Sir Andrew). Sir Toby also earns the ire of Malvolio. But Sir Toby has an ally, and eventually a mate, in Olivia's sharp-witted waiting-gentlewoman, Maria. Together they bring about the triumph of chaotic spirit, which Sir Toby embodies, and the ruin of the controlling, self-righteous Malvolio.

Maria   Olivia's clever, daring young waiting-gentlewoman. Maria is remarkably similar to her antagonist, Malvolio, who harbors aspirations of rising in the world through marriage. But Maria succeeds where

Malvolio fails—perhaps because she is a woman, but, more likely, because she is more in tune than Malvolio with the anarchic, topsy-turvy spirit that animates the play.

Sir Andrew Aguecheek A friend of Sir Toby's. Sir Andrew Aguecheek attempts to court Olivia, but he doesn't stand a chance. He thinks that he is witty, brave, young, and good at languages and dancing, but he is actually an idiot.

Antonio A man who rescues Sebastian after his shipwreck. Antonio has become very fond of Sebastian, caring for him, accompanying him to Illyria, and furnishing him with money—all because of a love so strong that it seems to be romantic in nature. Antonio's attraction to Sebastian, however, never bears fruit. Despite the ambiguous and shifting gender roles in the play, Twelfth Night remains a romantic comedy in which the characters are destined for marriage. In such a world, homoerotic attraction cannot be fulfilled.

CITY AND ISLINGTON
SIXTH FORM COLLEGE
283 - 309 GOSWELL ROAD
LONDON
EC1
TEL 020 7520 0652

ANALYSIS OF MAJOR CHARACTERS

VIOLA

Like most of Shakespeare's heroines, Viola is a tremendously likable figure. She has no serious faults, and we can easily discount the peculiarity of her decision to dress as a man, since it sets the entire plot in motion. She is the character whose love seems the purest. The other characters' passions are fickle: Orsino jumps from Olivia to Viola, Olivia jumps from Viola to Sebastian, and Sir Toby and Maria's marriage seems more a matter of whim than an expression of deep and abiding passion. Only Viola seems to be truly, passionately *in love* as opposed to being self-indulgently lovesick. As she says to Orsino, describing herself and her love for him:

> She pined in thought,
> And with a green and yellow melancholy
> She sat like patience on a monument,
> Smiling at grief. Was not this love indeed?
> (II.iv.111–114)

The audience, like Orsino, can only answer with an emphatic *yes*.

Viola's chief problem throughout the play is one of identity. Because of her disguise, she must be both herself and Cesario. This mounting identity crisis culminates in the final scene, when Viola finds herself surrounded by people who each have a different idea of who she is and are unaware of who she *actually* is. Were *Twelfth Night* not a comedy, this pressure might cause Viola to break down. Sebastian's appearance at this point, however, effectively saves Viola by allowing her to be herself again. Sebastian, who independent of his sister is not much of a character, takes over the aspects of Viola's disguise that she no longer wishes to maintain. Thus liberated by her brother, Viola is free to shed the roles that she has accumulated throughout the play, and she can return to being Viola, the woman who has loved and won Orsino.

ORSINO AND OLIVIA

Orsino and Olivia are worth discussing together, because they have similar personalities. Both claim to be buffeted by strong emotions, but both ultimately seem to be self-indulgent individuals who enjoy melodrama and self-involvement more than anything. When we first meet them, Orsino is pining away for love of Olivia, while Olivia pines away for her dead brother. They show no interest in relating to the outside world, preferring to lock themselves up with their sorrows and mope around their homes.

Viola's arrival begins to break both characters out of their self-involved shells, but neither undergoes a clear-cut change. Orsino relates to Viola in a way that he never has to Olivia, diminishing his self-involvement and making him more likable. Yet he persists in his belief that he is in love with Olivia until the final scene, in spite of the fact that he never once speaks to her during the course of the play. Olivia, meanwhile, sets aside her grief when Viola (disguised as Cesario) comes to see her. But Olivia takes up her own fantasy of lovesickness, in which she pines away—with a self-indulgence that mirrors Orsino's—for a man who is really a woman. Ultimately, Orsino and Olivia seem to be out of touch with real emotion, as demonstrated by the ease with which they shift their affections in the final scene—Orsino from Olivia to Viola, and Olivia from Cesario to Sebastian. The similarity between Orsino and Olivia does not diminish with the end of the play, since the audience realizes that by marrying Viola and Sebastian, respectively, Orsino and Olivia are essentially marrying female and male versions of the same person.

MALVOLIO

Malvolio initially seems to be a minor character, and his humiliation seems little more than an amusing subplot to the Viola-Olivia-Orsino love triangle. But he becomes more interesting as the play progresses, and most critics have judged him one of the most complex and fascinating characters in *Twelfth Night*. When we first meet Malvolio, he seems to be a simple type—a puritan, a stiff and proper servant who likes nothing better than to spoil other people's fun. It is this dour, fun-despising side that earns him the enmity of the zany, drunken Sir Toby and the clever Maria, who together engineer his downfall. But they do so by playing on a side of Malvolio that might have otherwise remained hidden—his self-regard and his remarkable ambitions, which extend to marrying Olivia and becoming, as he puts it, "Count Malvolio" (II.v.30).

When he finds the forged letter from Olivia (actually penned by Maria) that seems to offer hope to his ambitions, Malvolio undergoes his first transformation—from a stiff and wooden embodiment of priggish propriety into an personification of the power of self-delusion. He is ridiculous in these scenes, as he capers around in the yellow stockings and crossed garters that he thinks will please Olivia, but he also becomes pitiable. He may deserve his comeuppance, but there is an uncomfortable universality to his experience. Malvolio's misfortune is a cautionary tale of ambition overcoming good sense, and the audience winces at the way he adapts every event—including Olivia's confused assumption that he must be mad—to fit his rosy picture of his glorious future as a nobleman. Earlier, he embodies stiff joylessness; now he is joyful, but in pursuit of a dream that everyone, except him, knows is false.

Our pity for Malvolio only increases when the vindictive Maria and Toby confine him to a dark room in Act IV. As he desperately protests that he is *not* mad, Malvolio begins to seem more of a victim than a victimizer. It is as if the unfortunate steward, as the embodiment of order and sobriety, must be sacrificed so that the rest of the characters can indulge in the hearty spirit that suffuses *Twelfth Night*. As he is sacrificed, Malvolio begins to earn our respect. It is too much to call him a tragic figure, however—after all, he is only being asked to endure a single night in darkness, hardly a fate comparable to the sufferings of King Lear or Hamlet. But there is a kind of nobility, however limited, in the way that the deluded steward stubbornly clings to his sanity, even in the face of Feste's insistence that he is mad. Malvolio remains true to himself, despite everything: he *knows* that he is sane, and he will not allow anything to destroy this knowledge.

Malvolio (and the audience) must be content with this self-knowledge, because the play allows Malvolio no real recompense for his sufferings. At the close of the play, he is brought out of the darkness into a celebration in which he has no part, and where no one seems willing to offer him a real apology. "I'll be revenged on the whole pack of you," he snarls, stalking out of the festivities (V.i.365). His exit strikes a jarring note in an otherwise joyful comedy. Malvolio has no real place in the anarchic world of *Twelfth Night,* except to suggest that, even in the best of worlds, someone must suffer while everyone else is happy.

THEMES, MOTIFS & SYMBOLS

THEMES

Themes are the fundamental and often universal ideas explored in a literary work.

LOVE AS A CAUSE OF SUFFERING

Twelfth Night is a romantic comedy, and romantic love is the play's main focus. Despite the fact that the play offers a happy ending, in which the various lovers find one another and achieve wedded bliss, Shakespeare shows that love can cause pain. Many of the characters seem to view love as a kind of curse, a feeling that attacks its victims suddenly and disruptively. Various characters claim to suffer painfully from being in love, or, rather, from the pangs of unrequited love. At one point, Orsino depicts love dolefully as an "appetite" that he wants to satisfy and cannot (I.i.1–3); at another point, he calls his desires "fell and cruel hounds" (I.i.21). Olivia more bluntly describes love as a "plague" from which she suffers terribly (I.v.265). These metaphors contain an element of violence, further painting the love-struck as victims of some random force in the universe. Even the less melodramatic Viola sighs unhappily that "My state is desperate for my master's love" (II.ii.35). This desperation has the potential to result in violence—as in Act V, scene i, when Orsino threatens to kill Cesario because he thinks that Cesario has forsaken him to become Olivia's lover.

Love is also exclusionary: some people achieve romantic happiness, while others do not. At the end of the play, as the happy lovers rejoice, both Malvolio and Antonio are prevented from having the objects of their desire. Malvolio, who has pursued Olivia, must ultimately face the realization that he is a fool, socially unworthy of his noble mistress. Antonio is in a more difficult situation, as social norms do not allow for the gratification of his apparently sexual attraction to Sebastian. Love, thus, cannot conquer all obstacles, and those whose desires go unfulfilled remain no less in love but feel the sting of its absence all the more severely.

THE UNCERTAINTY OF GENDER

Gender is one of the most obvious and much-discussed topics in the play. *Twelfth Night* is one of Shakespeare's so-called transvestite comedies, in which a female character—in this case, Viola—disguises herself as a man. This situation creates a sexual mess: Viola falls in love with Orsino but cannot tell him, because he thinks she is a man, while Olivia, the object of Orsino's affection, falls for Viola in her guise as Cesario. There is a clear homoerotic subtext here: Olivia is in love with a woman, even if she thinks he is a man, and Orsino often remarks on Cesario's beauty, suggesting that he is attracted to Viola even before her male disguise is removed. This latent homoeroticism finds an explicit echo in the minor character of Antonio, who is clearly in love with his male friend, Sebastian. But Antonio's desires cannot be satisfied, while Orsino and Olivia both find tidy heterosexual gratification once the sexual ambiguities and deceptions are straightened out.

Yet, even at the play's close, Shakespeare leaves things somewhat murky, especially in the Orsino-Viola relationship. Orsino's declaration of love to Viola suggests that he enjoys prolonging the pretense of Viola's masculinity. Even after he knows that Viola is a woman, Orsino says to her, "Boy, thou hast said to me a thousand times / Thou never should'st love woman like to me" (V.i.260–261). Similarly, in his last lines, Orsino declares, "Cesario, come— / For so you shall be while you are a man; / But when in other habits you are seen, / Orsino's mistress, and his fancy's queen" (V.i.372–375). Even once everything is revealed, Orsino continues to address Viola by her male name. We can thus only wonder whether Orsino is truly in love with Viola, or if he is more enamoured of her male persona.

THE FOLLY OF AMBITION

The problem of social ambition works itself out largely through the character of Malvolio, the steward, who seems to be a competent servant, if prudish and dour, but proves to be, in fact, a supreme egotist, with tremendous ambitions to rise out of his social class. Maria plays on these ambitions when she forges a letter from Olivia that makes Malvolio believe that Olivia is in love with him and wishes to marry him. Sir Toby and the others find this fantasy hysterically funny, of course—not only because of Malvolio's unattractive personality but also because Malvolio is not of noble blood. In the class system of Shakespeare's time, a noblewoman would generally not sully her reputation by marrying a man of lower social status.

Yet the atmosphere of the play may render Malvolio's aspirations less unreasonable than they initially seem. The feast of Twelfth Night, from which the play takes its name, was a time when social hierarchies were turned upside down. That same spirit is alive in Illyria: indeed, Malvolio's antagonist, Maria, is able to increase her social standing by marrying Sir Toby. But it seems that Maria's success may be due to her willingness to accept and promote the anarchy that Sir Toby and the others embrace. This Twelfth Night spirit, then, seems to pass by Malvolio, who doesn't wholeheartedly embrace the upending of order and decorum but rather wants to blur class lines for himself alone.

Motifs

Motifs are recurring structures, contrasts, or literary devices that can help to develop and inform the text's major themes.

Letters, Messages, and Tokens

Twelfth Night features a great variety of messages sent from one character to another—sometimes as letters and other times in the form of tokens. Such messages are used both for purposes of communication and miscommunication—sometimes deliberate and sometimes accidental. Maria's letter to Malvolio, which purports to be from Olivia, is a deliberate (and successful) attempt to trick the steward. Sir Andrew's letter demanding a duel with Cesario, meanwhile, is meant seriously, but because it is so appallingly stupid, Sir Toby does not deliver it, rendering it extraneous. Malvolio's missive, sent by way of Feste from the dark room in which he is imprisoned, ultimately works to undo the confusion caused by Maria's forged letter and to free Malvolio from his imprisonment.

But letters are not the only kind of messages that characters employ to communicate with one another. Individuals can be employed in the place of written communication—Orsino repeatedly sends Cesario, for instance, to deliver messages to Olivia. Objects can function as messages between people as well: Olivia sends Malvolio after Cesario with a ring, to tell the page that she loves him, and follows the ring up with further gifts, which symbolize her romantic attachment. Messages can convey important information, but they also create the potential for miscommunication and confusion—especially with characters like Maria and Sir Toby manipulating the information.

MADNESS

No one is truly insane in *Twelfth Night,* yet a number of characters are accused of being mad, and a current of insanity or zaniness runs through the action of the play. After Sir Toby and Maria dupe Malvolio into believing that Olivia loves him, Malvolio behaves so bizarrely that he is assumed to be mad and is locked away in a dark room. Malvolio himself knows that he is sane, and he accuses everyone around him of being mad. Meanwhile, when Antonio encounters Viola (disguised as Cesario), he mistakes her for Sebastian, and his angry insistence that she recognize him leads people to assume that *he* is mad. All of these incidents feed into the general atmosphere of the play, in which normal life is thrown topsy-turvy, and everyone must confront a reality that is somehow fractured.

DISGUISES

Many characters in *Twelfth Night* assume disguises, beginning with Viola, who puts on male attire and makes everyone else believe that she is a man. By dressing his protagonist in male garments, Shakespeare creates endless sexual confusion with the Olivia-Viola-Orsino love triangle. Other characters in disguise include Malvolio, who puts on crossed garters and yellow stockings in the hope of winning Olivia, and Feste, who dresses up as a priest—Sir Topas—when he speaks to Malvolio after the steward has been locked in a dark room. Feste puts on the disguise even though Malvolio will not be able to see him, since the room is so dark, suggesting that the importance of clothing is not just in the eye of the beholder. For Feste, the disguise completes his assumption of a new identity—in order to be Sir Topas, he must look like Sir Topas. Viola puts on new clothes and changes her gender, while Feste and Malvolio put on new garments either to impersonate a nobleman (Feste) or in the hopes of becoming a nobleman (Malvolio). Through these disguises, the play raises questions about what makes us who we are, compelling the audience to wonder if things like gender and class are set in stone, or if they can be altered with a change of clothing.

MISTAKEN IDENTITY

The instances of mistaken identity are related to the prevalence of disguises in the play, as Viola's male clothing leads to her being mistaken for her brother, Sebastian, and vice versa. Sebastian is mistaken for Viola (or rather, Cesario) by Sir Toby and Sir Andrew, and then by Olivia, who promptly marries him. Meanwhile, Antonio mistakes Viola for Sebastian, and thinks that his friend has betrayed him when Viola claims to not know him. These cases of mistaken identity, common in Shakespeare's comedies, create the tangled situation that can be resolved only when Viola and Sebastian appear together, helping everyone to understand what has happened.

SYMBOLS

Symbols are objects, characters, figures, or colors used to represent abstract ideas or concepts.

OLIVIA'S GIFTS
When Olivia wants to let Cesario know that she loves him, she sends him a ring by way of Malvolio. Later, when she mistakes Sebastian for Cesario, she gives him a precious pearl. In each case, the jewel serves as a token of her love—a physical symbol of her romantic attachment to a man who is really a woman. The gifts are more than symbols, though. "Youth is bought more oft than begged or borrowed," Olivia says at one point, suggesting that the jewels are intended almost as bribes—that she means to buy Cesario's love if she cannot win it (III.iv.3).

THE DARKNESS OF MALVOLIO'S PRISON
When Sir Toby and Maria pretend that Malvolio is mad, they confine him in a pitch-black chamber. Darkness becomes a symbol of his supposed insanity, as they tell him that the room is filled with light and his inability to see is a sign of his madness. Malvolio reverses the symbolism. "I say this house is as dark as ignorance, though ignorance were as dark as hell; and I say there was never man thus abused" (IV.ii.40–42). In other words, the darkness—meaning madness—is not in the room with him, but outside, with Sir Toby and Feste and Maria, who have unjustly imprisoned him.

CHANGES OF CLOTHING
Clothes are powerful in *Twelfth Night*. They can symbolize changes in gender—Viola puts on male clothes to be taken for a male— as well as class distinctions. When Malvolio fantasizes about becoming a nobleman, he imagines the new clothes that he will have. When Feste impersonates Sir Topas, he puts on a nobleman's garb, even though Malvolio, whom he is fooling, cannot see him, suggesting that clothes have a power that transcends their physical function.

SUMMARY & ANALYSIS

ACT I, SCENES I–II

SUMMARY: ACT I, SCENE I

> *If music be the food of love, play on,*
> *. . .*
> *O spirit of love, how quick and fresh are thou. . . .*
> *(See* QUOTATIONS, *p. 49)*

In the land of Illyria, Duke Orsino enters, attended by his lords. Orsino is hopelessly in love with the beautiful Lady Olivia and pines away for her. He refuses to hunt and orders musicians to entertain him while he thinks about his desire for Olivia. His servant Valentine reminds him that Olivia does not return his love or even listen to the messages he sends her. We learn from Valentine that Olivia is in mourning for her brother, who has recently died. She wears a dark veil, and she has vowed that no one will see her face for another seven years—and she refuses to marry anyone until then. Orsino, obsessed with the woman who keeps refusing him, wants only to lie around on beds of flowers, listening to sweet music and dreaming of Olivia.

SUMMARY: ACT I, SCENE II

Meanwhile, on the Illyrian sea coast, a young noblewoman named Viola speaks with the captain whose crew has just rescued her from a shipwreck. Although Viola was found and rescued, her brother, Sebastian, seems to have vanished in the storm. The captain tells Viola that Sebastian may still be alive. He says that he saw Sebastian trying to keep afloat by tying himself to a broken mast. But Viola does not know whether or not it is worth holding onto hope. In the meantime, however, she needs to find a way to support herself in this strange land.

The ship's captain tells Viola all about Duke Orsino, who rules Illyria. Viola remarks that she has heard of this duke and mentions that he used to be a bachelor. The captain says that Orsino still is a bachelor, but then goes on to tell Viola about the Lady Olivia, whom the duke is courting. Again, we hear the tale of how Lady Olivia's brother died, leading her to cut herself off from the world. Viola expresses a wish that she could become a servant in the house of Olivia and hide herself away from the world as well. The captain responds that it is unlikely that Viola will enter Olivia's service because Olivia refuses to see any visitors, the duke included. Viola decides that, in that case, she will disguise herself as a young man and seek service with Duke Orsino instead. When she promises to pay him well, the captain agrees to help her, and they go off together in order to find a disguise for her.

ANALYSIS: ACT I, SCENES I–II

Viola's plan for disguising herself in Act I, scene ii introduces one of the central motifs of the play: disguise and the identity confusion related to it. Similarly, Orsino's mournful speech in Act I, scene i lets us know that the play will also concern matters of love: emotion, desire, and rejection. Put together, the two scenes suggest the extra twist that is the hallmark of *Twelfth Night*: mistaken gender identity. *Twelfth Night* is one of the plays referred to as Shakespeare's "transvestite comedies," and Viola's gender deception leads to all kinds of romantic complications.

The opening lines of *Twelfth Night,* in which a moping Orsino, attended by his servants and musicians, says, "If music be the food of love, play on," establish how love has conquered Orsino (I.i.1). His speech on this subject is rather complicated, as he employs a metaphor to try to establish some control over love. He asks for the musicians to give him so much music—the "food of love"—that he will overdose ("surfeit" [I.i.2]) and not be hungry for love any longer. Orsino's trick proves too simple, however; while it makes him tire of the music, it fails to stop him from thinking about love.

Orsino also makes a pertinent comment about the relationship between romance and imagination: "So full of shapes is fancy / That it alone is high fantastical" (I.i.14–15). This comment relates the idea of overpowering love ("fancy") to that of imagination (that which is "fantastical"), a connection that is appropriate for both Orsino and *Twelfth Night* as a whole. Beginning in this scene, the play repeatedly raises the question of whether romantic love has more to do with the person who is loved or with the lover's own imagination—whether love is real or merely something that the human mind creates for the sake of entertainment and delight. In the case of Orsino, the latter seems to be true, as he is less in love with Olivia herself than he is with the idea of being in love with Olivia. He claims to be devastated because she will not have him, but as the audience watches him wallow in his seeming misery, it is difficult to escape the impression that he is enjoying himself—flopping about on rose-covered beds, listening to music, and waxing eloquent about Olivia's beauty to his servants. The genuineness of Orsino's emotions comes into question even further when he later switches his affections from Olivia to Viola without a second thought; the audience then suspects that he does not care *whom* he is in love with, as long as he can be in love.

Meanwhile, Viola's decision to disguise herself as a young man in order to find a job seems somewhat improbable. Surely this elaborate ploy isn't necessary; even if Orsino only hires young men, there must be ladies other than Olivia in Illyria who are hiring servants. But Viola's act of disguising herself generates an endless number of interesting situations to advance the plot. Shakespeare's comedies frequently rely on similar improbabilities, ranging from absurd coincidences to identical twins. We can interpret Viola's disguise as something that makes the unprotected young woman feel safer in the strange land into which she has wandered. When she first describes her plan in this scene, she asks the ship's captain to disguise her as a eunuch—a castrated man. This part of the plan is never mentioned again, and Shakespeare seems to have changed his mind or forgotten about it: Viola later presents herself as simply a delicate young man. Still, the idea of a eunuch is important to the play, since it stands as yet another symbol of gender uncertainty.

In noting the gender confusion that pervades *Twelfth Night,* it is important to realize that, for Shakespeare's audiences, the idea of a girl successfully disguising herself as a boy wasn't as ludicrous as it might seem to us. In Shakespeare's day, *all* the parts in a play were acted by men: women weren't allowed to perform on the English stage until the late 1600s, more than half a century after Shakespeare flourished. Thus, every acting company included several delicate young boys, who played the female characters. Renaissance audiences were open to the idea that a young man could convincingly disguise himself as a woman, and vice versa. Such fluidity in portraying characters of either gender adds an extra dimension to the complexity of Shakespeare's cross-dressing characters.

SUMMARY & ANALYSIS

ACT I, SCENES III–IV

SUMMARY & ANALYSIS

SUMMARY: ACT I, SCENE III

In the house of Lady Olivia, we meet Olivia's uncle, Sir Toby Belch, and Olivia's waiting-gentlewoman, Maria. Sir Toby lives at Olivia's house and is cheerful, amusing, and usually tipsy. Maria warns Sir Toby that Olivia is annoyed by his drinking, but Sir Toby shrugs off this admonition. Maria also tells him that she has heard that he has brought a foolish friend to court Olivia: Sir Andrew Aguecheek, who shares Sir Toby's disreputable habits. Sir Toby protests that Sir Andrew is a perfect match for his niece, because he is very rich and is also accomplished in music and languages, but Maria doesn't care: in her view, Sir Andrew is a fool, a brawler, and a drunk.

Sir Andrew enters and, while Sir Toby is trying to introduce him to Maria, makes a fool of himself by repeatedly getting her name wrong. Evidently, Sir Andrew is a bumbling idiot. After Maria leaves, Sir Andrew and Sir Toby talk and joke like old friends. But Sir Andrew tells Sir Toby that he is discouraged and that he does not think that Olivia likes him. He plans to leave the next morning, and he remarks that Olivia will probably choose Orsino over him. Sir Toby persuades him to stay by flattering him. He says that Olivia will never marry "above her degree, neither in estate, years, nor wit," so Sir Andrew has a good chance with her (I.iii.90–91). Sir Toby compliments his friend's dancing and, through his encouragement, gets the vain and weak-minded—but good-hearted—Sir Andrew to show off his dancing skills.

SUMMARY: ACT I, SCENE IV

Meanwhile, at the house of Duke Orsino, Viola has adopted a new name—Cesario—to go with her new persona as a teenage boy. After only three days in Orsino's service, Cesario has already become a favorite of Orsino. Indeed, so much does Orsino favor his new servant that he insists on picking Cesario to go on his most important errand: to carry his messages of love to Olivia.

Cesario protests that Olivia, who has ignored Orsino for a long time, is not likely to start listening to his love messages now. But Orsino points out that Cesario is extremely young and handsome—so beautiful, in his lips and features, that he resembles a woman—and that Olivia is sure to be impressed by his attractiveness. Orsino tells Cesario to "act my woes" when he goes to see Olivia—to behave as if he shares Orsino's adoration for the noblewoman

(I.iv.25). After some discussion, Cesario reluctantly agrees to carry the message—reluctantly because, as she tells the audience in a quick aside, Viola herself has fallen in love with Orsino and wishes that she could be his wife.

ANALYSIS: ACT I, SCENES III–IV

Sir Toby, Sir Andrew, and Maria are *Twelfth Night*'s most explicitly comic characters, since they take themselves less seriously than the play's romantic leads. (Furthermore, the two noblemen's very names—"Belch" and "Aguecheek"—seem comically out of place.) These three provide amusement in different ways, however: Sir Toby seems to be an intelligent man and makes witty puns, to which the equally clever Maria is quick to respond. Sir Andrew Aguecheek, however, appears to be a fool. He doesn't understand Toby and Maria's wit, as we see when he is forced to ask Maria, "What's your metaphor?" and "[W]hat's your jest?" (I.iii.60–64). He is also easily flattered and doesn't realize certain painful truths—that he is not very witty, that Toby and Maria are making fun of him, and that he does not stand a chance with Olivia.

Act I, scene iv shows us the developing relationship between Orsino and Cesario. In another useful improbability, we find that, after only three days, Cesario has become a great favorite of the duke. As Orsino's servant Valentine tells Cesario, "If the Duke continues these favours towards you, . . . you are like to be much advanced" (I.iv.1–2). In the same conversation, Valentine assures Cesario that Orsino isn't fickle—that he remains steady and constant in his love. Since we have heard Orsino's flowery speeches about Olivia in Act I, scene i, we may question how sincere or steady his love really is, an uncertainty that grows as the play progresses.

Regardless, the way Orsino talks to Cesario makes it clear that Orsino likes Cesario very much—and his language is closer to that of romantic love than that of ordinary friendship. "Cesario," he tells him, "Thou know'st no less but all. I have unclasped / To thee the book even of my secret soul" (I.iv.11–13). Clearly, Orsino already seems to be attracted to Cesario in a way that defies our expectations of how male friends interact with one another.

This peculiar attraction is further developed when Orsino tells Cesario why he plans to send him to woo Olivia. Orsino explains that Olivia is more likely to listen to Cesario: "She will attend [Orsino's repeated messages of love] better in thy youth / Than in a nuncio's [i.e., messenger's] of more grave aspect" (I.iv.26–27). Cesario denies Orsino's claim, but Orsino tells him that he should believe it, because, in his youthfulness, Cesario is as pretty as a young woman. "Diana's lip / Is not more smooth and rubious [i.e., rosy]" than Cesario's, Orsino tells him, comparing him favorably to the goddess Diana; and Cesario's voice, Orsino claims, "[i]s as the maiden's organ, shrill and sound, / And all is semblative a woman's part" (I.iv.30–33). This series of compliments is both intriguing and complicated. In praising Cesario's attractiveness, Orsino tells Cesario that he looks like a woman. His interest in having Cesario go to Olivia suggests his belief that Cesario's womanly beauty will somehow entice Olivia. At the same time, it is difficult not to read in Orsino's words the suggestion that he too finds Cesario attractive: after all, Cesario reminds him strongly of a beautiful young woman.

ACT I, SCENE V

SUMMARY

> Make me a willow cabin at your gate
> And call upon my soul within the house
>
> . . .
> Cry out "Olivia!". . .

(See QUOTATIONS, p. 50)

In Olivia's house, Maria talks with Feste, Olivia's clown. Feste has been away for some time, it seems, and nobody knew where he was. Maria tells Feste that he will be in trouble with Olivia and that Olivia is likely to fire him. But, despite her threats not to stick up for him, Feste refuses to tell Maria where he has been.

Olivia arrives with Malvolio, the steward of her household. As Maria has anticipated, Olivia orders her servants to put Feste out of the house. But Feste, summoning up all his wit and skill, manages to put Olivia into a better mood. He asks her why she is mourning, and she answers that she is mourning for her brother. He says that he thinks her brother's soul is in hell, and she replies that he is in heaven. "The more fool, madonna, to mourn for your brother's soul, being in heaven," he says, and she responds approvingly (I.v.61–62). But Malvolio does not like Feste and asks coldly why Olivia wishes to keep a servant around who has no function except to poke fun at her. Olivia rebukes Malvolio for his "self-love" and says that Feste's insults are only "birdbolts" that do no damage (I.v.77–79).

Maria arrives with the message that there is a young man at the gate to see Olivia. (We know that this must be Viola, disguised as Cesario, bringing the message that Orsino gives her in Act I, scene iv.) It turns out that Sir Toby is currently talking to the young man, but Olivia sends Malvolio out to receive the messenger. Sir Toby comes in, obviously drunk (despite the early hour of the morning), and Olivia criticizes him for his alcoholism. Sir Toby goes out, and Olivia sends Feste to look after him.

Malvolio comes back, reporting that the young man refuses to leave the house until he has spoken with Olivia. Olivia asks Malvolio what the young man is like and receives the report that he is very young, handsome, and delicate-looking. Olivia is intrigued, and she decides to let the boy speak with her.

Viola, disguised as Cesario, is let in to see Olivia. Viola begins to deliver the love speech that Orsino gave her, but Olivia refuses to hear the memorized speech. Viola is eloquent enough to make Olivia pay attention to her, though, as she praises Olivia's great beauty and virtues to the skies. Olivia, increasingly fascinated by the messenger, begins to turn the conversation to questions about Cesario himself. Asking him about his parentage, she learns that Cesario comes from an aristocratic family (which, technically, is not a lie, since Viola's family is noble).

Olivia sends Cesario back to Orsino to tell him that Olivia still does not love him and never will. But she tells the young man to come back, if he wishes, and speak to her again about "how he [Orsino] takes it" (I.v.252). Then, after Cesario leaves, she sends Malvolio after him with a ring—a token of her attraction to Cesario—that she pretends Cesario left with her. Olivia, to her own surprise, finds that she has fallen passionately in love with young Cesario.

ANALYSIS: ACT I, SCENE V

At the beginning of Act I, scene v, we first meet Olivia's clown, Feste. (Feste's name is mentioned only once in the play; the stage directions usually refer to him simply as "Clown," while other characters call him "clown" or "fool.") Many noble households in the Renaissance kept a clown, and Shakespeare's comedies usually feature at least one. The fool's purpose was to amuse his noble masters and to tell the truth when no one else would think of telling it. The dual nature of the job meant that fools often pretended to be simpleminded when, in fact, most of them were skilled professionals and were highly intelligent.

SUMMARY & ANALYSIS

Feste embodies this duality: he spends much of his time making witty puns, as is expected, but he also has a sense of professionalism and of his own worth. As Feste says to Olivia when she orders him to be taken away, "Lady, '*Cucullus non facit monachum*'—that's as much to say as I wear not motley in my brain" (I.v.48–50). Feste means that his brightly colored clown's uniform—his "motley"—doesn't imply that he is any less intelligent than she is. Moreover, his ability to quote a Latin proverb on behalf of his argument reveals the depth of his learning. The Latin phrase means "The hood doesn't make the monk"—that is, what appears to be true is not always in harmony with what is true. Like Viola, then, Feste wears a kind of disguise: hers disguises her identity as a woman, while his conceals his true intelligence.

In this scene, we also meet both Olivia and her steward, Malvolio, for the first time. Malvolio has become, over time, perhaps the most famous character in *Twelfth Night*. He plays a small role in this scene, but he immediately attracts our attention because of how out of place he seems. In a comic play filled with ridiculous characters, Malvolio is serious and sour, with a distaste for amusement and laughter of any kind, as we see in his reaction to Feste. As the play goes on, the conflict between his temperament and that of the other characters—especially Sir Toby and Sir Andrew—comes out into the open, with extreme consequences.

Malvolio seems oddly matched with his mistress, given Olivia's emotionalism and her wild mood swings. When we first meet her, she is deep in mourning, but by the end of the scene, her grief gives way to a powerful infatuation with Cesario. In part, Shakespeare uses Olivia to portray romantic love as a kind of sickness that strikes people without warning. Love cannot be controlled; instead, it controls people. Olivia's sudden attraction to Cesario recalls the way Orsino talks about his love for Olivia in Act I, scene i. There, Orsino speaks of love as if it were a sickness that has overcome him, and then says that he has turned into a deer and "my desires, like fell and cruel hounds / E'er since pursue me" (I.i.21–22). In the same way, Olivia describes her sudden love for the handsome, young Cesario as a disease that has overwhelmed her. Just after Cesario leaves, she asks herself in confusion, "Even so quickly may one catch the plague? / Methinks I feel this youth's perfections / . . . / To creep in at mine eyes" (I.v.265–268).

Olivia's language, like Orsino's, reflects Renaissance ideas of courtly or romantic love: Olivia's and Orsino's descriptions of love—as a hunter, disease, or something willed by fate—echo ideas about romance that were common in Shakespeare's day. The same can be said of the language that Viola uses to describe Orsino's love for Olivia. For instance, Viola tells Olivia that Orsino loves her "[w]ith adorations, fertile tears, / With groans that thunder love, with sighs of fire" (I.v.274–275). Courtly ideals are also reflected in Viola's "willow cabin" speech in Act I, scene v (lines 237–245), in which she tells Olivia what she would do if she were the one trying to court Olivia. Viola says that she would build herself a house outside Olivia's gate, write Olivia love songs and sing them in the middle of the night, and call out Olivia's name until the hills and air echoed. This kind of romantic exaggeration was the kind of language often used by lovers and poets in Shakespeare's time.

Yet even as the play operates within the bounds of this tradition of courtly love, it also subverts it by showing how ridiculous it can be. After all, Viola's pretty speeches do not reflect her own thoughts but instead those of Orsino—and Orsino is really more in love with himself and his own inner life than he is with Olivia, as later scenes make clear. Furthermore, Olivia falls in love with Cesario after a few pretty speeches—but Cesario is really a woman who has herself fallen in love with Orsino in a matter of days! Thus, the play suggests that we should not take the various characters' romantic obsessions too seriously—they seem to come and go quickly and to be based less on real attraction than on self-indulgent emotionalism.

ACT II, SCENES I–II

SUMMARY: ACT II, SCENE I

Somewhere near the coast of Illyria, we meet two men who have not yet appeared in the play. One of them is called Antonio, and he has been hosting the other in his home. This other man is none other than Sebastian, the twin brother of Viola, who she believes has drowned. It seems that Antonio took Sebastian into his home when he washed up after the shipwreck and has been caring for him ever since. At first, Sebastian gave him a false name, but now that he plans to leave Antonio and go wandering, he decides to tell his benefactor his true identity and the tale of his sister, who he assumes drowned in their shipwreck. We learn here that Sebastian and Viola's father is long dead, and so Sebastian assumes that he has no family left. He is still devastated by the loss of his sister and is pre-

SUMMARY & ANALYSIS

paring to go wandering through the world, with little care as to what the future will hold.

Antonio urges Sebastian to let him come with him on his journey. It is clear that Antonio has become very fond of Sebastian and does not want to lose him. But Sebastian is afraid that his travels will be dangerous, and he urges Antonio to let him go alone. After Sebastian leaves to go to Orsino's court, Antonio ponders the situation: he wants to follow his friend and help him, but he has many enemies in Orsino's court and is afraid to go there. He cares about Sebastian so much, however, that he decides to face the danger and follow him to Orsino's court anyway.

SUMMARY: ACT II, SCENE II

Meanwhile, outside Olivia's house, Malvolio has caught up with Viola (still disguised as Cesario). Malvolio gives Cesario the ring that Olivia has sent with him, rebuking him for having left it with Olivia. Viola realizes Olivia's deception and plays along with it, pretending that she did indeed give the ring to Olivia. She tells Malvolio that Olivia took the ring and insists that Olivia must keep it.

Malvolio throws the ring onto the ground and exits. Alone, the confused Viola picks up the ring and wonders why Olivia has given it to her. She wonders if it means that Olivia has fallen in love with Cesario. If such is the case, Viola reflects, then events have indeed taken an ironic turn, because Olivia has unknowingly fallen in love with another woman. "Poor lady, she were better love a dream," Viola says to herself (II.ii.24). Apparently loved by Olivia and in love with Orsino, who loves Olivia, Viola expresses her hope that time will untangle these problems since she certainly cannot figure out how to solve them.

ANALYSIS: ACT II, SCENES I–II

It comes as no surprise to any reader of Shakespeare's comedies that Sebastian, Viola's twin brother, has turned up alive. His reappearance and resemblance to his sister (who, as we know, is currently disguised as a man) sets the stage for later mix-ups and mistaken identities, common elements in Shakespeare's comic plays.

The relationship between Antonio and Sebastian, meanwhile, though it is a minor part of the play, offers fertile ground for critical attention. Antonio and Sebastian are clearly close, dear friends. Yet the language Antonio uses, along with his behavior, suggests something even stronger. Antonio appears willing to sacrifice everything for his friend, giving up his time, money, and safety to follow and protect him. He begs Sebastian to let him be his servant and travel into danger with him, and Antonio decides to go even when he learns that Sebastian is headed for a dangerous place filled with Antonio's enemies. Moreover, Antonio's language carries a strong emotional charge: "If you will not murder me for my love, let me be your servant" (II.i.30–31). His implication that separation from Sebastian would be equivalent to a violent death demonstrates how deeply important to him his relationship with Sebastian is.

Powerful male friendships were more the norm in Shakespeare's day than in our own, and Antonio's language can be seen as simply the expression of a purely platonic passion. However, Antonio's words can also be seen as carrying an obvious homoerotic charge. It seems safe to say here that if Antonio were a woman, we would read her speech and actions as an unambiguous expression of her love for Sebastian and hope that he would return this love. In a play so concerned with bending gender roles—a play in which Orsino can seem to be attracted to Viola, for instance, even before she reveals herself to be a woman and not a man, and in which Olivia can fall for a man who is really a woman—Antonio's passion for Sebastian is erotic rather than platonic.

Leaving Antonio and Sebastian, the play returns to Viola, who is the central character in the action, and thus the only one who understands the entirety of the complicated love triangle. Orsino loves Olivia, who loves Viola, who in turn loves Orsino—but matters are hardly this simple, because both Orsino and Olivia are mistaken about Viola's real gender. Viola knows that romantic love, ideally, should lead to marriage. But in this particular triangle, there seems to be no hope of a resolution anywhere. Calling herself a "poor monster"—implying not that she is ugly but rather something not quite human, halfway between man and woman—Viola puts her finger on the problem (II.ii.32). Homoerotic love is not a real or final option in Shakespeare's comedies: as a man, Viola cannot win Orsino's love, but as a woman, she cannot return Olivia's. Finally giving herself up into the hands of fate, she says despairingly, "O time, thou must untangle this, not I. / It is too hard a knot for me t'untie" (II.ii.38–39). But fate—or, more accurately, the playwright—has already set the untangling forces in motion.

ACT II, SCENES III–IV

SUMMARY: ACT II, SCENE III

Sir Toby and Sir Andrew stay up late drinking in Olivia's house. Feste appears, and Sir Andrew compliments the clown on his singing. Both noblemen encourage Feste to sing another song. While he sings, Maria enters, warning them to keep their voices down or Olivia will call her steward, Malvolio, and tell him to kick them out. But the tipsy Sir Toby and Sir Andrew cheerfully ignore her.

Malvolio comes into the room. He criticizes the men for being drunk at all hours of the night and for singing so loudly. He warns Sir Toby that his behavior is intolerably rude and that, while Olivia is willing to let him be her guest (since he is her uncle), if Sir Toby does not change his behavior, he will be asked to leave. But Sir Toby, along with Sir Andrew and Feste, responds by making jokes and insulting Malvolio. After making a final threat, this one directed at Maria, Malvolio leaves, warning them all that he will let Olivia know about their behavior.

Sir Andrew suggests challenging Malvolio to a duel, but Maria has a better idea: to play a practical joke on him. As she explains to Sir Toby and Sir Andrew, Malvolio is a puritan, but at the same time his biggest weakness is his enormous ego: he believes that everybody loves him. Maria will use that weakness to get her revenge on him for spoiling their fun. Since Maria's handwriting is almost identical to Olivia's, Maria plans to leave letters lying around that will appear to have come from Olivia and will make Malvolio think that Olivia is in love with him.

Sir Toby and Sir Andrew are amazed by Maria's cleverness, and they admire the plan. Maria goes off to bed, planning to get started on her joke the next day. Sir Toby and Sir Andrew, deciding that it is now too late to go to sleep, head off to warm up more wine.

SUMMARY: ACT II, SCENE IV

> *There is no woman's sides*
> *Can bide the beating of so strong a passion*
> *As love doth give my heart....*
> *(See* QUOTATIONS, *p. 51)*

The next day, at Orsino's house, Orsino discusses love with his young page, Cesario (still Viola in disguise). Orsino tells Cesario that he can tell by looking at him that Cesario is in love. Since Viola

SUMMARY & ANALYSIS

is really in love with Orsino, Cesario admits that Orsino is right. When Orsino asks what the woman he loves is like, Cesario answers that she is very much like Orsino—similar to him in age and features. Orsino, not picking up on his page's meaning, remarks that Cesario would be better off loving a younger woman, because men are naturally fickle, and only a younger woman can keep them romantically satisfied for a long time.

Meanwhile, Orsino has sent for Feste, who apparently moves back and forth between the houses of Olivia and Orsino. Feste sings another very sad love song (this one about someone who dies for love), and, afterward, Orsino orders Cesario to go to Olivia again, pleading Orsino's love to her.

Cesario reminds Orsino that Olivia has denied his advances many times before, suggesting that Orsino accept that Olivia is not romantically interested in him, just as a woman in love with Orsino but whom Orsino did not love would have to accept *his* lack of interest in her. But Orsino says no woman can love with the same kind of passion as a man. Cesario disagrees and tells the story of a woman he knew who died for the love of a man: the woman never told the man about her love but, instead, simply wasted away. Cesario refers to this girl as her father's daughter—leading Orsino, naturally, to think that it must be Cesario's sister. He asks if the girl died of her love, and Viola answers ambiguously. Orsino then gives her a jewel to present to Olivia on his behalf, and she departs.

ANALYSIS: ACT II, SCENES III–IV

These scenes give us the first of the play's many songs. *Twelfth Night* is full of music, which is linked to romance from Orsino's command in the play's very first line: "If music be the food of love, play on" (I.i.1). Most of the songs are sung either by the drunken Sir Toby and Sir Andrew or by Feste the clown, who is a professional singer and entertainer as well as a joker. In Shakespeare's time, love was often associated with the emotional expressiveness of music, so the love songs in this comedy are quite appropriate.

The clash between Malvolio on the one hand and Sir Toby, Sir Andrew, and Maria on the other is a central conflict in *Twelfth Night*. On the face of things, it does not seem to be Malvolio's fault that he has to break up their party. After all, the men's drunken singing in their host's house in the middle of the night is unquestionably rude. But *Twelfth Night* is a play that ultimately celebrates chaos—whether it is brought on by romantic ardor, by alcohol, or simply by general enthusiasm—over the straitlaced order that Malvolio represents. The play's title refers to the Feast of the Epiphany, the twelfth day after Christmas, which in Shakespeare's England was a time for revelry and even anarchy—a day when servants impersonated their masters, alcohol flowed freely, and all of the customary social hierarchies were turned upside down. The puritanical, order-loving, and pleasure-hating spirit of Malvolio contrasts greatly with this anarchic spirit that flows through Sir Toby and Maria, Feste, and Sir Andrew. Malvolio, we realize, does not merely object to the circumstances of Sir Toby's revelry—he objects to revelry, music, and alcohol entirely. His sharp questions—"Do ye make an ale-house of my lady's house?" (II.iii.80–81)—prompt a bitter retort from Sir Toby, who asks. "Dost thou think because thou art virtuous, there shall be no more cakes and ale?" (II.iii.103–104). Sir Toby seems to understand Malvolio's attitude: because Malvolio himself detests merry-making, he thinks that no one should be allowed to make merry. His very name consists of elements—"Mal" and "volio"—that essentially mean, in Italian, "ill will," suggesting his profound contempt for others' pleasures.

Maria, however, proves more than a match for Malvolio. She knows his faults well: for one thing, he is a hypocrite, always trying to impress other people; worse, he is puffed up with pride, a weakness that she plans to take advantage of in exacting her revenge. Her comment that "it is his grounds of faith that all that look on him love him" (II.iii.134–135) remind us of Olivia's earlier comment that Malvolio is "sick of [meaning "sick with"] self-love" (I.v.77). Maria's trust in the all-consuming nature of Malvolio's egotism leads her to believe that it will be easy to make him think—foolishly—that Olivia loves him. The revenge seems appropriate—Malvolio, who loathes folly, will be tricked into displaying it.

The dialogue between Orsino and the disguised Viola in Act II, scene iv further develops the curious relationship between Orsino and his seemingly male servant. Their discussion of the relative power of men's and women's love is one of the most often-quoted passages in the play. The complicated ironies built into the scene— in which the audience knows that Cesario is really a woman in love with Orsino but Orsino remains unaware—add both a rich complexity and a sense of teasing to the discussions, even as the seeming hopelessness of Viola's position adds a hint of pathos. Still, one cannot find her plight too pathetic—the audience knows that the play is a comedy, in which romantic love must lead to married happiness.

Moreover, we have already heard Orsino's comments to Cesario in Act I, scene iv, praising Cesario's female-like beauty, so we know that Viola's disguise has not entirely prevented Orsino from being attracted to her.

Orsino's claim that men love more strongly than women was a commonplace one in Shakespeare's day, but Viola eloquently refutes it. In a very famous passage, she tells Orsino about how her fictional sister

> pined in thought,
> And with a green and yellow melancholy
> She sat like patience on a monument,
> Smiling at grief. . . .
>   (II.iv.111–114)

"Patience on a monument" refers to statues of the allegorical figure of Patience, which often adorned Renaissance tombstones. By comparing her imaginary sister to this stone figure, Viola subtly contrasts her own passion with the self-indulgent and grandiose lovesickness from which Orsino claims to suffer. She depicts herself as bearing a love that is, unlike the duke's, patient, silent, and eternally enduring. Of course, the image of a tombstone suggests that such a love is ultimately fatal, leading to Orsino's question—"But died thy sister of her love, my boy?" (I.iv.118). This question is appropriately left open: we do not know yet whether Viola will die (literally or metaphorically) of her love for Orsino, and so she can only respond, ambiguously yet cleverly, "I am all the daughters of my father's house, / And all the brothers too; and yet I know not" (I.iv.119–120). We, like Viola (and like Orsino), must wait to see how this tangle of desires and disguises will unravel.

Act II, scene v

Summary

> [E]very reason excites to this, that my lady loves me . . .
> a kind of injunction drives to these habits of her liking. .
> . .

> (See Quotations, p. 52)

In the garden of Olivia's house, Sir Toby, Sir Andrew, and Maria— along with Fabian, one of Olivia's servants—prepare to play their practical joke on Malvolio. Maria has written a letter carefully designed to trick him into thinking that Olivia is in love with him. She has been spying on him and knows that he is now approaching. She drops the letter in the garden path, where Malvolio will see it. She exits, while the three men hide among the trees and shrubbery.

Malvolio approaches on the path, talking to himself. He speaks of Olivia: it seems that he already thinks it possible that she might be in love with him. He is deep in a fantasy of what it would be like to be Olivia's husband and the master of her house. He would have power over all the other servants and even over Sir Toby. Sir Toby and the others can't help jeering at Malvolio's pride from their hiding place, but they do it softly so that he will not overhear them and realize that they are there.

Malvolio spots the letter lying in the garden path. He mistakes Maria's handwriting for Olivia's, as Maria has predicted, and Malvolio thinks that the letter is from Olivia. Apparently, Maria sealed the letter with Olivia's sealing ring to make the letter look even more authentic. To Sir Toby's pleasure, Malvolio decides to read it aloud.

The letter is addressed to "the unknown beloved" and contains what seems to be a riddle about love (II.v.92). It suggests that the writer is in love with somebody but must keep it a secret from the world, though she wants her beloved to know about it. The first part of the letter concludes by saying that the beloved's identity is represented by the letters M.O.A.I. Malvolio, naturally, works over the message in his mind until he has made it mean that he is the beloved (he notes, for instance, that all four of the letters appear in his own name). Sir Toby and the rest laugh at him from behind the bush.

Once he has convinced himself that Olivia is in love with him, Malvolio reads the second half of the letter. The mysterious message implies that the writer wishes to raise Malvolio up from his position of servitude to one of power. But the letter also asks him to show the writer that he returns her love through certain signs. The letter orders him to wear yellow stockings, "go cross-gartered" (that is, to wear the straps of his stockings crossed around his knees), be sharp-tempered with Sir Toby, be rude to the servants, behave strangely, and smile all the time. Jubilantly, Malvolio vows to do all these things in order to show Olivia that he loves her in return.

After Malvolio leaves, Sir Toby remarks that he "could marry this wench [Maria] for this device. . . . And ask no other dowry with her but such another jest" (II.v.158–160). Maria then rejoins the men, and she, Sir Toby, and Fabian have a good laugh, anticipating what Malvolio is likely to do now. It turns out that Olivia actually hates the color yellow, can't stand to see crossed garters, and doesn't want anybody smiling around her right now, since she is still officially in mourning. In other words, Malvolio is destined to make a great fool of himself. They all head off together to watch the fun.

ANALYSIS: ACT II, SCENE V

The practical joke played on Malvolio raises themes which, by now, are familiar: the instability of identity, the importance of clothing in establishing one's identity and position, and the illusions and delusions that we let ourselves fall into in the name of love. Like everyone else, from Orsino to Viola, Malvolio falls victim to the allure of romance. Despite his outward puritanism, he is as much a romantic as anyone—although his fantasy of marrying Olivia has as much to do with class-related ambition as it does with infatuation.

Malvolio's desire to rise above his class spurs his self-delusion, but it also explains why Sir Toby and the others find his fantasy so ludicrous. Malvolio is an unsuitable match for Olivia not only because of his unattractive personality but also because he is not of noble blood. He is a commoner, while Olivia is a gentlewoman. As such, that Malvolio would imagine Olivia marrying him seems obscene to them. We may recall how interested Olivia is earlier to find out from young Cesario, on whom she has a crush, that he is a "gentleman"—meaning that he is of noble birth (I.v.249). In the class system of Shakespeare's time, it would have seemed very strange for a noblewoman to marry below her rank.

Significantly, Malvolio's fantasy of becoming Olivia's husband involves changing his clothing: he imagines himself "in my branched velvet gown"—the garb of a wealthy noblemen, not of a steward (II.v.42–43). The letter also asks him to alter his clothing at the same time that he changes his personality. Just as the cross-dressing habits of Viola, the play's central character, suggest a link between clothes and gender roles, so Malvolio's ideas about what he will wear as an aristocrat suggest a connection between wardrobes and social hierarchies. Outward appearances, it seems, can shape reality—or so Malvolio imagines. Of course, just as Viola remains a woman beneath her clothes, Malvolio's fantasies of velvet gowns and yellow stockings will do nothing to change his place in society.

Maria's riddle, in which she plays with the letters of Malvolio's name, is meant to be both obvious and ambiguous. Clearly, Malvolio is supposed to decide that it refers to him, but it also allows us to watch him wrench the evidence around to arrive at the conclusion at which he so desperately wants to arrive. Various critics have wondered whether there is any further meaning in the letters M.O.A.I., other than their obvious status as letters pulled out of Malvolio's name, but no widely accepted answers have been put forward.

Malvolio's comments upon recognizing what seems to be Olivia's handwriting, however, do contain an obscene pun—about which Malvolio is evidently not supposed to be aware. Examining her handwriting, he notes, "[T]hese be her very c's, her u's, and her t's, and thus makes she her great P's" (II.v.78–79). C-U-T, or "cut," was a Renaissance slang term for the vagina, and "thus makes she her great P's" strongly suggests a reference to penises.

ACT III, SCENES I–III

SUMMARY: ACT III, SCENE I

Viola, still in disguise as Cesario, has returned to Lady Olivia's house to bring her another message of love from Orsino (the errand that Orsino sends Cesario on at the end of Act II, scene iv). Outside Olivia's house, Cesario meets Feste, the clown. Feste jokes and makes puns with him. Cesario jokes with comparable skill and good-naturedly gives Feste some coins for his trouble. Feste goes inside to announce the arrival of Cesario to Olivia.

Sir Toby and Sir Andrew arrive in the garden and, meeting Cesario for the first time, make some rather awkward conversation with him. The situation is made awkward by the fact that Sir Andrew behaves foolishly, as usual, and both men are slightly drunk. Sir Toby invites Cesario into the house, but before they can enter, Olivia comes down to the garden, accompanied by Maria. She sends everyone else away in order to listen to what Cesario has to say.

Once alone with Cesario, Olivia suddenly begs him not to give her any more love messages from Orsino. She lets Cesario know how deeply in love with him she is. Cesario tells Olivia as politely as he can that he cannot love her. Olivia seems to accept this rejection, but she realizes privately that she cannot so easily get rid of her love for this beautiful young man, even if he scorns her. Cesario swears to Olivia that no woman shall ever be mistress of his heart and turns to go. But Olivia begs him to come back again, suggesting desperately that maybe Cesario can convince her to love Orsino after all.

SUMMARY & ANALYSIS

SUMMARY: ACT III, SCENE II

Back in Olivia's house, Sir Andrew tells Sir Toby that he has decided to leave. He says that he has seen Olivia fawning over Cesario in the orchard, and he seems to realize at last that Olivia is not likely to marry him. But Sir Toby—who wants to keep Andrew around because he has been spending Sir Andrew's money—tells Sir Andrew that he ought to stay and show off his manliness for her. Fabian helps Sir Toby in his persuasion, assuring Sir Andrew that Olivia might only have been teasing him and trying to make him jealous. Sir Andrew agrees, and Sir Toby encourages him to challenge Cesario to a duel, in order to prove his love for Olivia.

Maria comes in and reports that Malvolio is behaving like an absolute ass—he has been doing everything that the letter has asked him to do. He is wearing yellow stockings and crossed garters and will not stop smiling—all in all, he is more ridiculous than ever before. Sir Toby and Fabian eagerly follow Maria to see what is going on.

SUMMARY: ACT III, SCENE III

Elsewhere, in the streets of Illyria, we find that Sebastian and Antonio have at last arrived at their destination. We learn that Antonio is not safe in Illyria: it seems that Duke Orsino's men are hostile to him, for many years ago Antonio was involved in a sea fight against Orsino in which he did them much damage. But Antonio's love for Sebastian has caused him to defy the danger and come with Sebastian to Illyria.

Sebastian is not yet tired, so he and Antonio agree that Antonio find lodging for the two of them at an inn. Sebastian, meanwhile, will roam the streets, taking in the sights of the town. Knowing that Sebastian doesn't have much money, Antonio gives Sebastian his purse so that Sebastian can buy himself something if he spots a trinket he likes. They agree to meet again in an hour at the inn.

ANALYSIS: ACT III, SCENES I–III

Once again we meet Feste the clown, and once again we notice that beneath his nonsense, he is obviously intelligent. In fact, Viola is inspired to comment on this after her conversation with Feste: "This fellow is wise enough to play the fool, / And to do that well, craves a kind of wit," she notes (III.i.53–54). She realizes that a good clown must be able to judge the personalities and moods of all the people with whom he interacts, and to know when to talk, what to say, and when to keep quiet. Her remark that "[t]his is a practice / As full of labour as a wise man's art" (III.i.58–59) reminds us of Feste's earlier comments about his own professionalism: "Well, God give them wisdom that have it; and those that are fools, let them use their talents" (I.v.13–14). There is an irony here—Feste is skilled as a fool, yet he is also one of the play's most intelligent characters.

Olivia's character, meanwhile, has undergone a startling shift. When we first meet her, she is deep in mourning, dismissive of romantic love, and somewhat close in spirit to the dour Malvolio. Indeed, her early grief seems as self-indulgent as Orsino's lovesickness. But Viola has won Olivia over; she has replaced her grief with infatuation, and Olivia now willingly gives herself over to the zany shamelessness that fills the play. She behaves in a remarkably forward fashion in these scenes: when they are speaking alone, for instance, she takes Cesario's hand—a very unusual action for a noblewoman to perform. By the end of the scene, Olivia is reduced to begging Cesario to come back again, saying that perhaps she will change her mind about Orsino after all. Passion has conquered dignity and order, at least in Olivia's heart.

Of course, while Viola has broken the spell of grief and has convinced Olivia to give herself over to romantic desire, she herself cannot fulfill Olivia's yearnings. She can only reply "I pity you" (III.i.115) to the noblewoman's pleadings, and offer vague explanations for her rejection of Olivia—"I have one heart, one bosom, and one truth, / And that no woman has, nor never none / Shall mistress be of it save I alone" (III.i.148–151). Her reliance on rather abstract terms ("one heart," "one truth") reflects the emotional distance that she maintains from Olivia.

Antonio's love for Sebastian, meanwhile, remains as strong as ever, as he risks his life to pursue Sebastian. His remark that he follows Sebastian out of his "desire, / More sharp than filèd steel" (III.iii.4–5) has the same violently passionate twinge as his earlier comparison of separation from Sebastian with "murder" (II.i.30). He seeks also to protect Sebastian, owing to his "jealousy [i.e., worry] what might befall your travel, / . . . in these parts . . . / . . . / Rough and unhospitable" (III.iii.8–11).

Antonio's attachment to Sebastian comprises not only concern for his safety but also a willingness to spend money on him (he even entrusts his purse to him). "[Y]our store / I think is not for idle markets, sir," Antonio tells Sebastian, a statement with a double meaning (III.iii.45–46). The more apparent meaning is that Sebastian doesn't have enough money to spend on trivial things, but the words also suggest that Sebastian is too good to spend time with just any-

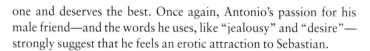

one and deserves the best. Once again, Antonio's passion for his male friend—and the words he uses, like "jealousy" and "desire"—strongly suggest that he feels an erotic attraction to Sebastian.

ACT III, SCENE IV

SUMMARY

Olivia, who sent a servant after the departing Cesario to persuade him to return, tries to figure out how to woo him to love her. Feeling suddenly melancholy, Olivia sends for Malvolio because she wants someone solemn and sad to help with her strategy.

But when Malvolio appears, he behaves very strangely. He wears crossed garters and yellow stockings, smiles foolishly, and continually quotes strange phrases that Olivia does not recognize. Malvolio, we quickly realize, is quoting passages from the letter that he believes Olivia wrote to him. He suddenly exclaims things like "Remember who commended thy yellow stockings . . . And wished to see thee cross-gartered" (III.iv.44–47). Olivia, of course, knows nothing about the letter and thinks Malvolio has gone mad. When the news arrives that Cesario has returned, she assigns Maria and Sir Toby to take care of Malvolio, and goes off to see Cesario.

Malvolio is convinced—in spite of Olivia's apparent bewilderment—that he is correct in his surmises and that Olivia is really in love with him. But when Sir Toby, Fabian, and Maria come to see him, they pretend to be certain that he is possessed by the devil. Malvolio, remembering the letter's advice that he speak scornfully to servants and to Sir Toby, sneers at them and stalks out. Delighted by the turn the events have taken, they decide together to lock Malvolio into a dark room—a frequent treatment for people thought to be possessed by devils or madmen. Sir Toby realizes that since Olivia already thinks Malvolio is crazy, he can do whatever he wants to the unfortunate steward.

Sir Andrew enters with a letter challenging the young Cesario to a duel. Sir Toby privately decides that he will not deliver the silly letter but, instead, will walk back and forth between Sir Andrew and Cesario. He will tell each that the other is fearsome and out for the other's blood. That, he decides, should make for a very funny duel.

Cesario comes back out of the house, accompanied by Olivia, who insists that Cesario take a locket with her picture as a love token. She bids he come again the next day, and then goes back inside. Sir Toby approaches Cesario, delivering Sir Andrew's challenge and telling him what a fierce fighter Sir Andrew is. Cesario says that he does not wish to fight and prepares to leave. Sir Toby then returns to Sir Andrew and tells his friend that Cesario is a tremendous swordsman, anxious for a fight. When Andrew and Cesario cross paths, though, Sir Toby tells each of them that the other has promised not to draw blood in the duel. Reluctantly, the two draw their swords and prepare for a fight.

Suddenly, Antonio enters. He sees Cesario and mistakes him for his beloved Sebastian, and tells Sir Andrew that he, Antonio, will fight Sir Andrew in Sebastian's place. Several Illyrian officers burst onto the scene. They have recognized Antonio—a wanted man in Illyria—and arrest him. Antonio, realizing that he will need to pay a bail bond in order to free himself, asks Cesario, whom he still believes is Sebastian, to return his purse (which Antonio gives to Sebastian in Act III, scene iii). Viola, however, has no idea who Antonio is. Antonio thinks that Sebastian is betraying him by pretending not to know him, and he is heartbroken. Deeply shocked and hurt, he rebukes Sebastian. The officers, thinking Antonio is insane, take him away. Viola is left with a sudden feeling of hope: Antonio's mention of someone named "Sebastian" gives her some hope that her own brother—whom she has thought dead—is in fact alive and nearby. Viola runs off to look for him, leaving Sir Andrew and Sir Toby very confused.

ANALYSIS

The plot speeds up in this scene, and the cases of mistaken identity and deception become increasingly complicated. First, we see the hilarious results of Maria's deception, which bears fruit in Malvolio's alleged madness. Because he thinks that he shares a secret understanding with Olivia, Malvolio expects her to understand the bizarre things he does and says. Olivia, of course, is bewildered by the change in her normally somber steward, and his apparently illogical responses to her questions make her assume, naturally enough, that he must be out of his mind. She interprets his quotations from the letter as simple insanity: "Why, this is very midsummer madness," she says after listening to a string of them (III.iv.52). But Malvolio, cut off from reality, willfully ignores these signs that all may not be as he thinks. He fits Olivia's words to his mistaken understanding of the situation. When she refers to him as "fellow," for instance, he takes the term to mean that she now thinks more highly of him than she has before (III.iv.57). His earlier egotism and self-regard has become pure, self-centered delusion, in which everything that happens can be interpreted as being favorable to him. As he puts it, "[N]othing that can be can come between me and the full prospect of my hopes" (III.iv.74–75). Malvolio makes a simple mistake—he twists facts to suit his beliefs rather than adapting his beliefs to the facts.

At this point, we realize why Maria's letter was such a work of genius: in ordering Malvolio to be rude to Sir Toby and the servants, she makes certain that Malvolio will refrain from explaining himself to anyone. Thus, Maria has orchestrated matters such that Malvolio's behavior will be the justification for the others' treatment of him as if he were possessed. Sir Toby, with mock-bravery, says that if "Legion himself possessed [Malvolio], yet I'll speak to him" (III.iv.78–79). Later, Sir Toby and the servants decide to treat Malvolio "gently, gently," a recommended manner of dealing with people thought to be possessed. Once Malvolio leaves, the three plot to "have him in a dark room and bound"—another common treatment for madmen (III.iv.121). As Sir Toby notes, Olivia already thinks that Malvolio is mad, so they can torture him until they grow tired of it. It is here that we begin to feel pity for Malvolio. His humiliation may be richly deserved, but there is a kind of overkill in Sir Toby and Maria's decision to lock him away. He seems to be punished cruelly for what are, after all, minor sins, and our sense that Malvolio is being wronged only increases in Act IV.

Sir Toby's trickery in frightening Cesario and Sir Andrew with fearsome tales about each other's prowess sets the stage for yet another wrinkle in the web of deception. Viola, who has been in disguise throughout the play, is now mistaken for yet a third person—her own brother, Sebastian. Antonio's mistake is made much more poignant by his badly timed arrest and his grief and anger at thinking that Sebastian has stolen his money and betrayed him. He tells Viola, who is disguised as Cesario but who he thinks is Sebastian, that her beautiful features conceal a wickedness of soul: "In nature there's no blemish but the mind. / None can be called deformed but the unkind" (III.iv.331–332). His anguish here is touching—far more touching than the flowery grief of Olivia, say, or the lovesick posturings of Orsino. It moves us because we know that for Antonio there can be no happy endings. A comedy like *Twelfth Night* ends, inevitably, with marriages—but there is no one for Antonio to marry, since he loves only Sebastian.

Meanwhile, Antonio's mistaken insistence that Sebastian knows him and owes him money causes his arresting officers to think that Antonio, in turn, is insane. The disguises, secret identities, and crossed lines of communication lead to humorous circumstances, but they also tinge the action with hints of insanity and tragedy. Antonio is arrested, and Malvolio is confined as a madman—and the audience begins to feel that things are going too far. In the world of *Twelfth Night*, disorder and the gentle madness of romantic infatuation are celebrated, but there is a limit to how much anarchy can dominate the stage before comedy gives way to tragedy. As in a tragedy, everything in *Twelfth Night* falls into disorder as the play moves toward the conclusion; because the play is a comedy, however, we know that matters will be put right in the end.

ACT IV, SCENES I–III

SUMMARY: ACT IV, SCENE I

Near Olivia's house, Feste the clown comes across the person who he thinks is Cesario and tries to bring him to Olivia's house. This individual, however, is actually Viola's twin brother, Sebastian. Sebastian, of course, is confused by Feste's claims to know him. Sir Toby and Sir Andrew then find them. Sir Andrew, thinking that Sebastian is the same person he was about to duel a few minutes before, attacks him. But Sebastian, unlike Viola, is a scrappy fighter, and starts to beat Sir Andrew with his dagger, leading the foolish nobleman to cry for mercy. The bewildered Sebastian wonders if he is surrounded by madmen and tries to leave. But Sir Toby grabs him to prevent him from going. The two exchange insults, and Sebastian and Sir Toby draw their swords and prepare to fight.

Suddenly, Olivia enters. She sees Sir Toby preparing to fight the person who she thinks is Cesario. Angrily, she orders Sir Toby to put away his sword and sends away all the others. She begs Cesario to come into her house with her. Sebastian is bewildered, but Olivia does not give him time to think, and the still-confused Sebastian agrees to follow her, saying, "If it be thus to dream, still let me sleep!" (IV.i.59).

SUMMARY: ACT IV, SCENE II

Inside Olivia's house, Maria, Sir Toby, and the other servants have locked Malvolio into a small, dark chamber. Maria asks Feste to put on the robes of a clergyman and pretend to be Sir Topas, a fictional curate, or priest. Sir Toby and Maria then send Feste to talk to the imprisoned Malvolio in the voice of Sir Topas while they listen in on the conversation.

Pretending to be the priest, Feste addresses Malvolio, who cannot see him inside his prison. Malvolio tells Feste that he is not insane, and Malvolio begs Feste to get him out of the locked room. But Feste deliberately misunderstands and misleads the steward. He tells Malvolio that the room is not actually dark but is full of windows and light and that Malvolio must be mad or possessed if he cannot see the brightness. Malvolio denies Feste's claims, and he urges Feste to question him in the hopes of proving his sanity. But Feste uses ridiculous questions and then contradicts the steward's answers. He concludes by telling Malvolio he is still mad and must remain in the darkness.

Sir Toby and Maria are delighted by the joke but are also tiring of it. Sir Toby is worried that Olivia, already offended by his drinking and carousing, might catch him in this prank. They send Feste back to Malvolio, where Feste—now using both his own voice and that of Sir Topas, as if the two are having a conversation—speaks to Malvolio again. Malvolio swears he isn't crazy, and begs for paper, ink, and light with which to write a letter to Olivia. Feste promises to fetch him the items.

SUMMARY: ACT IV, SCENE III

Elsewhere in the house, Sebastian is wandering, dazed yet happy. He is very confused: he doesn't seem to be insane, and yet a beautiful woman—Olivia—has been giving him gifts and wants to marry him. He wishes he could find Antonio to discuss the situation with him. He states, however, that when he went back to their inn, Antonio was nowhere to be seen. Olivia now returns with a priest, asking Sebastian (who she still thinks is Cesario) if he is still willing to marry her. Sebastian happily agrees, and they go off to get married.

ANALYSIS: ACT IV, SCENES I–III

Sebastian briefly takes center stage in these scenes, but he fails to make much of an impression as a character in his own right: his principal role is to serve as a male substitute for his resourceful and attractive twin sister, Viola. Sebastian's primary state of mind in these scenes is total confusion, which is understandable. Having arrived in a country that he has never seen before, he is suddenly surrounded by people who seem to think they know him and who have extreme attitudes toward him: some want to kill him, while others appear to be in love with him. It is not surprising that, after trying to fend off the insistent Feste and being abruptly attacked by Sir

Andrew, Sebastian asks in bewilderment, "Are all the people mad?" (IV.i.24). Olivia's approach forces him to wonder about his own state of mind: "Or I am mad, or else this is a dream" (IV.i.57). These references to insanity are significant. As he does with Antonio and Malvolio, Shakespeare suggests here that madness and the chaos associated with comedy are closely linked.

By Act IV, scene iii, however, Sebastian begins to come to terms with his situation. He decides that the sun that he sees is real, as are the air that he breathes and the pearl that Olivia has given him. "[T]hough 'tis wonder that enwraps me thus, / Yet 'tis not madness," he decides (IV.iii.3–4). He even reasons out the situation with the beautiful woman who claims to love him. If Olivia were mad, he figures, surely her servants wouldn't obey her—so she must be sane. All the same, he realizes, "There's something in't / That is deceivable" (IV.iii.20–21). He is right, of course; he just hasn't figured out yet exactly what the deception is.

Meanwhile, issues of madness and identity are addressed in a different way in the dialogue between Feste and the unfortunate Malvolio. In this scene, Feste proves himself a master of disguise by imitating the curate's voice and speech patterns. But there is something very strange in his disguise: there seems no reason for Feste to dress up in a priest's robes if Malvolio, locked in the darkness as he is, cannot even see him. Again, as with Viola's male clothes and Malvolio's fantasies about wearing a nobleman's garments, Shakespeare seems to suggest a link between garments and identity. To impersonate Sir Topas, Feste *must* dress like him, so closely are clothes and public personae bound together.

Feste also uses tactics of confusion on poor Malvolio, telling him outright lies to make him think his senses deceive him and, thus, trying to make Malvolio himself believe that he is insane. He adds the final insult after Malvolio angrily claims that he is as sane as Feste himself, telling Malvolio, "Then you are mad indeed, if you be no better in your wits than a fool" (IV.ii.82–83). Again, we are impressed with Feste's cleverness; yet, as he torments Malvolio, we begin to wonder if he is employing his talents to a good end. The steward, whose earlier humiliation is perhaps well deserved, now seems a helpless victim. It is as if Malvolio, as the embodiment of order and sobriety, must be sacrificed so that the rest of the characters can indulge in the topsy-turvy spirit of the Feast of the Twelfth Night that suffuses the play.

Malvolio is hardly a tragic figure. After all, he is only being asked to endure a single night in darkness. But he earns our respect, nevertheless, as he stubbornly clings to his sanity, even in the face of Feste's insistence that he is mad. Malvolio, perhaps more than anyone else in this frenetic, zany play, *knows* that he is sane, and he will not allow the madness swirling in the air of Olivia's home to destroy his sense of his own sanity. One cannot help pitying him, in spite of his flaws. He seems to be punished for not being as mad as everyone else, more than he is for any real sin. He cries, "I say this house is as dark as ignorance, though ignorance were as dark as hell; and I say there was never man thus abused," making the darkness of his prison a powerful symbol for the madness that seems to have taken over the world of the play (IV.ii.40–42). Malvolio is right—but being right avails him nothing. *Twelfth Night* is a play filled with absurdity and madcap fun, and Malvolio suffers his unhappy fate because he is unable to put his scruples, his puritanism, and his pride aside to join in the revelry.

ACT V, SCENE I

SUMMARY

> If this be so . . .
> . . .
> 　　　　　　　　　　　　　 Give me thy hand,
> And let me see thee in thy woman's weeds.
> 　　　　　　　　　 (See QUOTATIONS, p. 53)

Orsino approaches Olivia's house, accompanied by Viola (still disguised as Cesario) and his men. The Illyrian law officers come in looking for Orsino, dragging Antonio. Orsino, who fought against Antonio long ago, recognizes him as an honorable enemy. He asks Antonio what caused him to come into Orsino's territory, where Antonio knew he would be in danger. Antonio responds by telling the story of how he rescued, befriended, and protected Sebastian, traveling with him to this hostile land. He lashes out at Cesario, whom he continues to mistake for Sebastian, claiming that Sebastian has stolen his purse and denied knowing him. Viola and Orsino are both bewildered, for Viola truly does not know Antonio.

Olivia enters and speaks to Cesario, she too believing him to be Sebastian, whom she has just married (at the end of Act IV, scene iii). Orsino, angry at Cesario's apparent betrayal of him, threatens to carry Cesario off and kill him. Viola, resigned, prepares to go with

Orsino to her death and says that she loves only him. Olivia is shocked, believing that her new spouse is betraying her. She calls in the priest, who, thinking that the young man in front of him is Sebastian, testifies that he has just married Olivia to the young man. Orsino orders Olivia and Cesario to leave together and never to appear in his sight again.

Suddenly, Sir Andrew enters, injured and calling for a doctor. He says that he and Sir Toby have just been in a fight with Orsino's servant, Cesario. Seeing Cesario, Sir Andrew accuses him of the attack, but the confused Viola answers that she is not responsible. Olivia orders Sir Andrew and Sir Toby away for medical attention.

Finally, Sebastian appears, apologizing to Olivia for having beaten up Sir Toby and Sir Andrew. Recognizing Antonio, and not yet seeing his sister, Sebastian cries out joyfully how glad he is to see him. Dazed, all the others stare at Sebastian and Viola, who finally see one another. They interrogate one another with a barrage of questions about their birth and family history. Finally, they believe that they have each found their lost sibling. Viola excitedly tells Sebastian to wait until she has put her woman's clothing back on— and everyone suddenly realizes that Cesario is really a woman.

Orsino, realizing that Olivia has married Sebastian, doesn't seem terribly unhappy at losing her. Turning back to Viola, he reminds her that, disguised as a boy, she has often vowed her love to him. Viola reaffirms her love, and Orsino asks to see her in female garb. She tells him that her clothes were hidden with a sea captain, who now has taken service with Malvolio. Suddenly, everybody remembers what happened to Malvolio. Feste and Fabian come in with Malvolio's letter, delivered from his cell. At Olivia's order, Feste reads it aloud. Malvolio writes that the letter seemingly written to him by Olivia will explain his behavior and prove he is not insane.

Realizing that Malvolio's writing does not seem like that of a crazy man, Olivia orders that he be brought to them. Malvolio is brought in, and he angrily gives Olivia the letter that Maria forged, demanding to know why he has been so ill treated. Olivia, recognizing Maria's handwriting, denies having written it but understands what must have happened. Fabian interrupts to explain to everyone how—and why—the trick was played. He mentions in passing that Sir Toby has just married Maria. Malvolio, still furious, vows revenge and leaves abruptly. Orsino sends someone after Malvolio to make peace and find Viola's female garments. He then announces that the double wedding will be celebrated shortly. Everyone exits except Feste, who sings one last song, an oddly mournful melody about growing up and growing old, and the play ends.

ANALYSIS

This long scene concludes the action of the play. A few at a time, the play's main characters enter until they are all in the same place at the same time, and the various confusions and deceptions can finally be resolved. Of course, the ultimate climax is the reunion of Sebastian and Viola—their meeting unravels the major deceptions and conflicts of the play.

The moment before the climax, significantly, is the most complicated moment in the entire play for Viola, at least in terms of how everyone understands her identity. Just before Sebastian's entrance, Viola, in her disguise as Cesario, is surrounded by many people, each of whom has a different idea of who she is and *none* of whom knows who she *actually* is. Sebastian's entrance at this point effectively saves Viola from her identity crisis. We might think of the scene as showing Sebastian taking over the aspects of Viola's disguise that she no longer needs to wear. It is Sebastian whom Antonio has really been seeking, Sebastian who has really married Olivia, and, in the end, Sebastian who is actually male. Thanks to her brother's assumption of these roles, Viola is free to cast off her masculine disguise. First she casts it off through speech, as she lets everyone know that she is really a woman, and then through deed, as she talks about putting back on her women's clothing, or "maiden weeds" (V.i.248).

But even once the truth about Viola's womanhood comes out, the uncertainty that her disguise has raised remains. For instance, Orsino's declaration of love to Viola is strangely phrased. Continuing to address Viola as if she were male, he says, "Boy, thou hast said to me a thousand times / Thou never shouldst love woman like to me" (V.i.260–261). Similarly, in his final lines Orsino declares,

> Cesario, come—
> For so you shall be while you are a man;
> But when in other habits you are seen,
> Orsino's mistress, and his fancy's queen.
> (V.i.372–375)

Orsino continues to address his future wife by her assumed male name, which hints at his ongoing attachment to Viola's masculine potential. Though he knows Viola is a woman, he continues to recognize Cesario as a legitimate identity for Viola. His statement that in female garb Viola will be his queen does not make it clear that he is asking Viola to renounce her assumed male identity forever; nor is it clear whether Orsino is truly in love with Cesario or Viola.

Equally puzzling, but in a different way, is Orsino's earlier threat to kill Cesario when he thinks his servant has betrayed him. "I'll sacrifice the lamb that I do love," he says, and Viola acquiesces meekly (V.i.128). "And I, most jocund, apt, and willingly, / To do you rest, a thousand deaths would die," she declaims (V.i.130–131). These bizarre speeches—articulating Orsino's strange violence and Viola's apparent death wish—recede into the background amid the general rejoicing that follows, but they leave critics baffled. Perhaps Shakespeare is suggesting that love is so close to madness that both Orsino and Viola can easily tip over the edge into blood-drenched insanity, where one lover becomes a killer and the other a sacrificial lamb.

Meanwhile, the general happiness that prevails is marred by the reemergence of Malvolio from his dark prison. When the trick is revealed, no one else seems to be quite as upset about it as the steward. "Alas, poor fool, how have they baffled thee!" Olivia says to him, calling the resolutely unfoolish Malvolio a "fool" (V.i.358). This barb, at once, adds insult to injury and shows how the spirit of the play has upended even the steadfast, puritanical steward. The unamused Malvolio's parting remark—"I'll be revenged on the whole pack of you"—sounds a jarring note in the supposedly tranquil, joyful concluding scene (V.i.365). Malvolio's anger injects a hint of pathos or realism into the otherwise idyllic ending: someone must suffer while everyone else is happy. Antonio is likewise sacrificed to the anarchic spirit of the play, although less noticeably: his homosexual ardor for Sebastian must go unsatisfied in a play where heterosexual marriage is the logical endpoint.

For those who feel a sense of disquiet and ambivalence amid the joy of the conclusion, Feste's closing song seems to provide some support. The song is the last of many musical numbers in the play, and it is also one of the most melancholy, recounting a story of growing up to discover the harshness and unkindness of life. Comedy and romantic bliss triumph in *Twelfth Night,* but through characters like Malvolio and Feste, Shakespeare leaves us with a feeling of unease. Like the feast that gives the play its name, *Twelfth Night* is festive and joyful—but all feast days must come to an end, the concluding song suggests, and give way to the "wind and the rain" of life (V.i.387).

IMPORTANT QUOTATIONS EXPLAINED

1. If music be the food of love, play on,
    Give me excess of it that, surfeiting,
    The appetite may sicken and so die.
    That strain again, it had a dying fall.
    O, it came o'er my ear like the sweet sound
    That breathes upon a bank of violets,
    Stealing and giving odour. Enough, no more,
    'Tis not so sweet now as it was before.
    [Music ceases]
    O spirit of love, how quick and fresh art thou
    That, notwithstanding thy capacity
    Receiveth as the sea, naught enters there,
    Of what validity and pitch so e'er,
    But falls into abatement and low price
    Even in a minute! So full of shapes is fancy
    That it alone is high fantastical.
        (I.i.1–15)

The play's opening speech includes one of its most famous lines, as the unhappy, lovesick Orsino tells his servants and musicians, "If music be the food of love, play on." In the speech that follows, Orsino asks for the musicians to give him so much musical love-food that he will overdose ("surfeit") and cease to desire love any longer. Through these words, Shakespeare introduces the image of love as something unwanted, something that comes upon people unexpectedly and that is not easily avoided. But this image is complicated by Orsino's comment about the relationship between romance and imagination: "So full of shapes is fancy / That it alone is high fantastical," he says, relating the idea of overpowering love ("fancy") to that of imagination (that which is "fantastical"). Through this connection, the play raises the question of whether romantic love has more to do with the reality of the person who is loved or with the lover's own imagination. For Orsino and Olivia, both of whom are willing to switch lovers at a moment's notice, imagination often seems more powerful than reality.

2.   Make me a willow cabin at your gate
      And call upon my soul within the house,
      Write loyal cantons of contemnèd love,
      And sing them loud even in the dead of night;
      Hallow your name to the reverberate hills,
      And make the babbling gossip of the air
      Cry out 'Olivia!' O, you should not rest
      Between the elements of air and earth
      But you should pity me.
          (I.v.237–245)

Viola (in her disguise as Cesario) delivers this speech to Olivia after Orsino has sent her to carry his messages of love to Olivia. In this speech, however, Cesario sets aside the prepared messages and instead tells Olivia what he would do if he were in love with her. This speech is significant, then, because it sets the stage for Olivia's infatuation with the person she thinks is Cesario: instead of helping win Olivia for Orsino, Cesario's passionate words make Olivia fall in love with him. This development is understandable, when one considers what Viola says here—she insists that she would be outside Olivia's gate night and day, proclaiming her love, until Olivia took "pity" on her. This kind of devotion contrasts sharply with the way Orsino actually pursues his courtship of Olivia: instead of planting himself outside her door and demonstrating his devotion, he prefers to remain at home, lolling on couches and complaining of his broken heart. The contrast, then, between the devotion that Viola imagines here and the self-involvement that characterizes Orsino's passion for Olivia, suggests that Viola has a better understanding than Orsino of what true love should be.

3.   There is no woman's sides
         Can bide the beating of so strong a passion
         As love doth give my heart; no woman's heart
         So big, to hold so much. They lack retention.
         Alas, their love may be called appetite,
         No motion of the liver, but the palate,
         That suffer surfeit, cloyment, and revolt.
         But mine is all as hungry as the sea,
         And can digest as much. Make no compare
         Between that love a woman can bear me
         And that I owe Olivia.
              (II.iv.91–101)

Orsino speaks these words as he discusses his love for Olivia with Cesario. Here, he argues that there can be no comparison between the kind of love that a man has for a woman and the kind of love that women feel for men. Women, he suggests, love only superficially—in the "palate," not the "liver," implying that for men love is somehow deeper and less changeable. While his love is constant, he insists, a woman's love suffers "surfeit, cloyment, and revolt." This speech shows the extent of Orsino's self-involvement by demonstrating that he cares only about his own emotions and assumes that whatever Olivia feels, it cannot "compare" to his own feelings for her. But there is also an irony here, since Orsino ascribes qualities to women's love that actually apply to his own infatuations. He claims that women love superficially and can have their feelings change easily; in fact, later in the play, he happily transfers his affections from Olivia to the revealed-as-female Viola. It is the woman, Viola, whose love for Orsino remains constant throughout. Indeed, Viola answers this speech by citing herself as an example of a woman who remains constant in love (without revealing that she is talking about herself, of course). Thus, given what the audience sees onstage, Orsino's opinions about love seem to be wrong on almost every count.

QUOTATIONS

4. Daylight and champaign discovers not more. This is open. I will be proud, I will read politic authors, I will baffle Sir Toby, I will wash off gross acquaintance, I will be point-device the very man. I do not now fool myself, to let imagination jade me; for every reason excites to this, that my lady loves me. She did commend my yellow stockings of late, she did praise my leg, being cross-gartered, and in this she manifests herself to my love, and with a kind of injunction drives to these habits of her liking. I thank my stars, I am happy. I will be strange, stout, in yellow stockings, and cross-gartered, even with the swiftness of putting on. Jove and my stars be praised.

(II.v.140–150)

Malvolio speaks these words after he finds the letter written by Maria that seems to reveal that Olivia is in love with him. Until this point, Malvolio has seemed a straitlaced prig with no enthusiasms or desires beyond decorum and an orderly house. Here we see his puritanical exterior is only a veneer, covering powerful ambitions. Malvolio dreams of being loved by Olivia and of rising in the world to become a nobleman—both of these dreams seem to be fulfilled by the letter. For the audience, this scene is tremendously comic, since we can easily anticipate that Malvolio will make a fool of himself when he follows the letter's instructions and puts on yellow stockings and crossed garters. But there is also a hint of pathos in Malvolio's situation, since we know that his grand ambitions will come crashing down. Our pity for him increases in later scenes, when Sir Toby and Maria use his preposterous behavior to lock him away as a madman. Malvolio is not exactly a tragic figure; he is too absurd for that. But there is something at least pitiable in the way the vanity he displays in this speech leads to his undoing.

5.   ORSINO: If this be so, as yet the glass seems true,
         I shall have share in this most happy wrack.
         [To VIOLA] Boy, thou hast said to me a
         thousand times
         Thou never shouldst love woman like to me.

      VIOLA: And all those sayings will I overswear,
         And all those swearings keep as true in soul
         As doth that orbèd continent the fire
         That severs day from night.

      ORSINO: Give me thy hand,
         And let me see thee in thy woman's weeds.
         (V.i.258–266)

This exchange follows the climax of the play, when Sebastian and
Viola are reunited, and all the misunderstandings are cleared up.
Here, Orsino ushers in a happy ending for his long-suffering Viola
by declaring his willingness to wed her. This quote thus sets the stage
for general rejoicing—but it is worth noting that even here, the
gender ambiguities that Viola's disguise has created still persist. Orsino knows that Viola is a woman—and a woman, apparently,
to whom he is attracted. Yet he addresses her as "Boy" in this
speech, even as he is accepting her vows of love. This incident is not
isolated: later, Orsino continues to call his new betrothed "Cesario," using her male name. This odd mode of address raises, and
leaves unanswered, the question of whether Orsino is in love with
Cesario, the beautiful young man, or with Viola, the beautiful
young woman.

QUOTATIONS

CITY AND ISLINGTON
SIXTH FORM COLLEGE
283 - 309 GOSWELL ROAD
LONDON
EC1
TEL 020 7520 0652

KEY FACTS

FULL TITLE
Twelfth Night, or What You Will

AUTHOR
William Shakespeare

TYPE OF WORK
Play

GENRE
Comedy

LANGUAGE
English

TIME AND PLACE WRITTEN
Between 1600 and 1602, England

DATE OF FIRST PUBLICATION
1623, in the First Folio

PUBLISHER
Isaac Jaggard and Edward Blount

TONE
Light, cheerful, comic; occasionally frantic and melodramatic, especially in the speeches of Orsino and Olivia

TENSE
Present (the entire story is told through dialogue)

SETTING (TIME)
Unknown

SETTING (PLACE)
The mythical land of Illyria (Illyria is a real place, corresponding to the coast of present-day Albania—but *Twelfth Night* is clearly set in a fictional kingdom rather than a real one)

PROTAGONIST
Viola

KEY FACTS

MAJOR CONFLICT

Viola is in love with Orsino, who is in love with Olivia, who is in love with Viola's male disguise, Cesario. This love triangle is complicated by the fact that neither Orsino nor Olivia knows that Viola is really a woman.

RISING ACTION

The mounting confusion, mistaken identities, and professions of love leading up to Act V

CLIMAX

Sebastian and Viola are reunited, and everyone realizes that Viola is really a woman

FALLING ACTION

Viola prepares to marry Orsino; Malvolio is freed and vows revenge; everyone else goes off to celebrate

THEMES

Love as a cause of suffering; the uncertainty of gender; the folly of ambition

MOTIFS

Letters, messages, and tokens; madness; disguises; mistaken identity

SYMBOLS

Olivia's gifts; the darkness of Malvolio's prison; changes of clothing

FORESHADOWING

Little or none, as the play moves too fast.

STUDY QUESTIONS & ESSAY TOPICS

STUDY QUESTIONS

1. *Disguises and changes of clothing are central to the plot of Twelfth Night. Which characters in the play spend time in disguise, and how is this thematically important?*

Many people in *Twelfth Night* assume a disguise of one kind or another. The most obvious example is Viola, who puts on the clothing of a man and makes everyone believe that she is a male. This disguise causes great sexual confusion, as a bizarre love triangle results in which Viola is in love with Orsino, who loves Olivia—who loves Cesario, the male identity that Viola assumes. Thus, by dressing his protagonist in male garments, Shakespeare shows how malleable and self-delusional human romantic attraction can be.

Another character in disguise is Malvolio, who dresses oddly (in crossed garters and yellow stockings) in the hope of winning Olivia. In his case, the change of clothing suggests his belief that altering his wardrobe can lead to an alteration of his social status. When he dreams of being Olivia's husband, he imagines himself above all in a different set of clothes, suggesting that class and clothing are inextricably linked. Later, after Malvolio has been declared mad and has been confined to a dark room, Feste, pretending to be the fictional priest Sir Topas in order to deceive Malvolio, puts on a disguise—even though Malvolio will not be able to see him since the room is so dark. This scene is particularly suggestive: Feste's desire to wear a disguise even though his victim won't see it implies that the link between clothes and reality goes deeper than mere appearances. For Feste, at least, the disguise makes the man—in order to be Sir Topas, he must look like Sir Topas. Ultimately, then, Shakespeare raises questions about human identity and whether such classifications as gender and class status are fixed entities or can be changed with a simple shift of wardrobe.

2. *Twelfth Night, the holiday after which the play is
    named, was celebrated as a festival in which everything
    was turned topsy-turvy, with traditional social roles and
    behavior temporarily suspended. Are things similarly
    turned upside down in Illyria?*

One could argue that normal situations are turned upside down in
Illyria in several ways. First, there is the prevalence of disguise and
the ambiguity of gender roles. The central character in this regard is
the protagonist, Viola. After she arrives on Illyrian shores, she takes
on the disguise of a young man, thus at once concealing her identity
and reversing her normal gender role. This reversal leads to a most
confusing love life, in which she winds up loving a man and being
loved by a woman who do not realize that she is a woman.

Meanwhile, the play also depicts attempts to alter the established
systems of class and authority. Malvolio, for instance, dreams of
marrying Olivia and gaining authority over his social superiors,
such as Sir Toby. The servants, whom Malvolio does command, get
authority over Malvolio himself by being able to lock him in the
dark room as a madman. Meanwhile, Malvolio's antagonist,
Maria, succeeds where he fails by managing to marry Sir Toby and
thereby rising from her common birth to a noble rank. Indeed, Malvolio's difficulties seem to stem from his unwillingness to be abnor-
mal enough. He dreams of escaping the rigid class system that
makes him a servant, but otherwise he is a paragon of respectability
and proper behavior. These qualities, in the topsy-turvy world of the
play, cause his downfall, because they earn him the enmity of Sir
Toby and Maria. Finally, all these events take place within a setting
in which madness and anarchy are everywhere—Sir Toby's drunk-
enness and disruptive behavior, Malvolio's supposed insanity,
Feste's clowning, and the general perplexity caused by the doubling
of Viola and Sebastian. All in all, the play is permeated with a sense
of joyful confusion, in which nothing can be taken for granted.

QUESTIONS & ESSAYS

3.   *How is romantic love depicted in the play? What points
     does Shakespeare seem to be making about romance?*

Despite *Twelfth Night*'s comic action and happy ending, Shakespeare paints an ambiguous picture of romance and infatuation in
the play. Love is generally represented as something sudden and
irresistible, something that attacks its victim from the outside in a
fashion similar to a disease. Like a disease, love is extremely difficult
to get rid of or cure. People seem to suffer painfully from it—or at
least they claim to suffer. Orsino describes it as an "appetite" that
must be satisfied (I.i.1–3); Olivia calls love a "plague" (I.v.265);
Viola sighs that "[m]y state is desperate for my master's love"
(II.ii.35). Because love makes those who suffer from it desperate, it
has the potential to result in violence, as in Act V, scene i, when Orsino, thinking that Cesario is Olivia's lover, threatens to kill him. At
this point, the play is only a few delicate steps away from turning
into a tragedy—a testament to how violent and terrible the power of
love can be.

   At the same time, however, Shakespeare subverts these images of
love as a terrible disease or appetite, suggesting that it may not be as
serious as characters like Olivia and Orsino think. Both of them
tend to be melodramatic and self-centered, and both seem more
interested in *being in love* than in any particular love interest. This
egotism is apparent in how readily the two switch the objects of
their affection near the play's close: Orsino loses Olivia but happily
takes up with Viola, while Olivia gladly exchanges a pretend man,
Cesario, for a real one in Sebastian. The ease with which these supposedly lovesick characters jump from one love interest to another
suggests that love may be more of a game than anything else—and
that, like everything else in *Twelfth Night,* it should not be taken
too seriously.

QUESTIONS & ESSAYS

SUGGESTED ESSAY TOPICS

1. Discuss the role of mistaken identity in TWELFTH NIGHT. Who is mistaken for whom, and what do these mix-ups signify?

2. Discuss the role of the explicitly comic characters—Sir Toby, Sir Andrew, Feste, and Maria. What function do they serve? How is each one different from the others? How is Feste, in particular, different from Sir Toby and Sir Andrew?

3. What role does Malvolio serve in the play? Does his fate seem unjust? Is it out of place in a romantic comedy? If so, why might Shakespeare have included it?

4. Paying particular attention to the fate of Malvolio and Antonio, discuss how Shakespeare brings some ambiguous touches to the happy ending.

5. Compare Orsino and Olivia, and discuss how their attitudes about strong emotions are similar or different. What does Shakespeare suggest about the nature of love and other powerful feelings in his portrayal of these two characters?

REVIEW & RESOURCES

QUIZ

1. Who is Orsino in love with at the beginning of the play?

   A. Olivia
   B. Viola
   C. Maria
   D. Malvolio

2. Complete the quote: "If music be the food of _____, play on."

   A. Sleep
   B. Sorrow
   C. Love
   D. Joy

3. Where does Twelfth Night take place?

   A. England
   B. Illyria
   C. Ruritania
   D. Denmark

4. Why is Olivia unwilling to receive any visitors?

   A. She is hideously deformed
   B. She is terribly shy
   C. She cannot speak
   D. She is in mourning for her dead brother

5. How does Viola come to be at Orsino's court?

   A. She is shipwrecked nearby
   B. She is captured and made a slave
   C. She is invited to be a guest of Orsino
   D. She is Orsino's daughter

REVIEW & RESOURCES

6. Why is Sir Andrew Aguecheek staying at Olivia's home?

  A. He is her uncle
  B. He is trying to court Maria
  C. He is trying to court Olivia
  D. He is Malvolio's brother

7. How does Viola disguise herself?

  A. She puts on makeup to make herself resemble an old woman
  B. She dresses like a man
  C. She shaves her head and wears a false beard
  D. She does not disguise herself

8. What is Malvolio's position?

  A. He is Orsino's fool
  B. He is Viola's butler
  C. He is Sir Toby's butler
  D. He is Olivia's steward

9. What is Sir Toby's great vice?

  A. He is a drunkard
  B. He is a glutton
  C. He enjoys pornography
  D. He has no vices

10. Who does Orsino send to carry his messages to Olivia?

  A. Malvolio
  B. Feste
  C. Viola, disguised as Cesario
  D. Sebastian

11. Who does Viola fall in love with?

  A. Malvolio
  B. Orsino
  C. Sir Toby
  D. Olivia

12. Who does Olivia fall in love with?

    A. Orsino
    B. Malvolio
    C. Antonio
    D. Viola, in her disguise as Cesario

13. Who is Sebastian?

    A. Viola's brother
    B. Orsino's cousin
    C. Olivia's fool
    D. Malvolio's son

14. Who forges the letter that Malvolio thinks is from Olivia?

    A. Feste
    B. Sir Toby
    C. Maria
    D. Viola

15. What does the forged letter make Malvolio believe?

    A. That Maria is in love with him
    B. That he is going to inherit a fortune
    C. That Viola is in love with him
    D. That Olivia is in love with him

16. Who takes care of Sebastian after he is shipwrecked?

    A. Viola
    B. Feste
    C. Malvolio
    D. Antonio

17. Who challenges Cesario to a duel?

    A. Orsino
    B. Sir Andrew
    C. Malvolio
    D. Antonio

18. What does Malvolio wear in the hope of pleasing Olivia?

    A. Green leggings
    B. Women's clothing
    C. Yellow stockings and crossed garters
    D. A red wig and silver pantaloons

19. Why does Antonio travel to Illyria?

    A. To be close to Sebastian
    B. To get revenge on Orsino
    C. To woo Olivia
    D. He does not travel

20. Why does Sir Andrew try to fight with Sebastian?

    A. He thinks that Sebastian has killed Orsino
    B. He thinks that Sebastian wants to kill Sir Toby
    C. He thinks that Sebastian is in love with Maria
    D. He thinks that Sebastian is Cesario

21. What do Sir Toby and the others do to Malvolio?

    A. They kill him
    B. They lock him in a dark room and tell him he is mad
    C. They tar and feather him
    D. They get him drunk and convince him to sing with them

22. What disguise does Feste wear when he speaks with Malvolio?

    A. Cesario
    B. Olivia
    C. Sir Topas, the curate
    D. An angel

23. Who does Olivia marry?

    A. Sebastian
    B. Antonio
    C. Orsino
    D. Malvolio

REVIEW & RESOURCES

24. When he realizes that Cesario is a woman, what does Orsino do?

    A. He orders her executed
    B. He banishes her
    C. He betroths her to Antonio
    D. He decides to marry her

25. Which character does not get married (or plan to) at the end of the play?

    A. Orsino
    B. Sir Toby
    C. Sebastian
    D. Malvolio

ANSWER KEY:
1: A; 2: C; 3: B; 4: D; 5: A; 6: C; 7: B; 8: D; 9: A; 10: C;
11: B; 12: D; 13: A; 14: C; 15: D; 16: D; 17: B; 18: C; 19: A;
20: D; 21: B; 22: C; 23: A; 24: D; 25: D

SUGGESTIONS FOR FURTHER READING

BLOOM, HAROLD, ed. *Modern Critical Interpretations of* TWELFTH NIGHT. New York: Chelsea House, 1987.

———. *Shakespeare: The Invention of the Human.* New York: Riverhead Books, 1998.

BOOTH, STEPHEN. "Twelfth Night 1.1: The Audience as Malvolio." In *Shakespeare's Rough Magic: Essays in Honor of C. L. Barber,* ed. Peter Erickson and Coppélia Kahn. Newark: University of Delaware Press, 1985. 149–167.

GAY, PENNY. "Twelfth Night: Desire and Its Discontents." In *As She Likes It: Shakespeare's Unruly Women.* London: Routledge, 1994. 17–47.

GREENBLATT, STEPHEN, gen. ed. *The Norton Shakespeare* (Based on the Oxford Edition). New York and London: W.W. Norton & Co., 1997.

KING, WALTER N., ed. *Twentieth-Century Interpretations of* TWELFTH NIGHT. Englewood Cliffs, New Jersey: Prentice Hall, 1968.

LEGGATT, ALEXANDER. TWELFTH NIGHT: *Shakespeare's Comedy of Love.* London: Methuen, 1974.

WELLS, STANLEY, ed. TWELFTH NIGHT: *Critical Essays.* New York: Garland, 1986.